GOD'S OP
(ROYAL PRIESTHOOD SERIES)

BY
REV. DAVID PETERSON

PUBLISHED BY
KRATOS PUBLISHER

God's Opinion

Copyright ©2022 by REVEREND DAVID PETERSON

Published by: Kratos Publisher

Content

Introduction

2 Samuel 6:20-21.

When David returned home to bless his family, Michal the daughter of Saul came out to meet him. She said in disgust, how distinguished the king of Israel looks today. Shamelessly exposing himself to the servant girls as any vulgar person might do. David reported to Michal, I was dancing before the Lord, who chose me above your father, and all his family. He appointed me as the leader of Israel, the people of the Lord. So I celebrate before the Lord.

I love that scripture. But, before I sink my teeth into that particular part of the segment, I want to backtrack just a little bit into the life of David. A lot of people know David's most popular story, about him defeating Goliath who was a giant, the whole army of Israel was afraid, there is no doubt that this guy was massive. He was somebody that you wouldn't want to meet in a dark alley or you wouldn't want to get into a fight with our pub, or in the queue to get popcorn at the cinema. But David, being a man that walked with God, had a strong and tight relationship with the Lord. He wasn't afraid to take on Goliath. A lot of people might affirm that he was crazy. He was beside himself. He had lost the plot, but David was only focused on the opinion of God and he said to himself, If God can deliver me from a bear, if He can deliver me from a lion, surely, He will deliver me from this giant. It came to a point when David approached the king and said, I want to take him on. I believe I have the power like Anthony Joshua to take down this giant. I believe I have the anointing to handle this crisis. And the Bible speaks about Saul giving David his garments to wear, and his armour. But David said I want to be myself. I want to be free. I know how I took out the bear and the lion. It wasn't with all these armours. Sometimes people want to fit you into a box and say, you should be like this. You should talk like this, have your hair like this and like that. You should talk like this. Just say, I want to focus on the opinion of God because it's God's opinion about you that will stand the test of time. It is God's opinion about you that will last forever. People change. One minute, they're clapping for you, the next minute, they're deleting you on Facebook and blocking you on Instagram. Jesus experienced the same thing. One minute they were saying Hosanna in the highest, Hosanna in the highest. Next, they were saying, crucify him. But God kept His opinion about Jesus all way through and said this is my son whom I love. So, looking at David, he stood before the giant and it's a popular story. We know that God was there for him. He took his slingshot by turning it around, hit the giant in his forehead with the stone, and the giant collapsed. God was there for him because, he focused on the opinion of God even though everybody was afraid, and thought that it was impossible.

Everybody said this is just a young boy that came out of nowhere. Who is he? How can he come from the backside of the desert, from just tending sheep in the bushes somewhere to be taking on this giant, and protecting the whole nation?

You Can Be More

Don't limit yourself, walk in who God sees you to be. Focus on God's opinion of you. You might have an opinion about yourself and think I'm nothing, I've failed so many times, I've made so many outlandish mistakes, but, God's opinion of you; once you've come before him, confessed and spoken to him, you're washed clean.

He can use you to do great things. David focused on the opinion of God and he said, regardless of what everybody else thinks, I want to stand up for this nation and say, God, I'm going to walk in whom you say that I am.

Acknowledge God in All

Looking at the scripture that was read earlier, David's wife was upset because of the way he expressed how much he loved God before the whole nation. Sometimes in life, you just have to express how much you love God irrespective of what people think about you because it's His opinion that matters the most. A lot of people, when I was growing up in Sunday school and youth groups said to me, Oh, David danced until his clothes fell off. I used to think, wow, that's amazing. The guy was born naked. But when I did research, and after finishing my degree in theology, I learned along the way that he dance until his kingly robes fell off.

Sometimes in life, no matter what you achieve, no matter how far you get, regardless of how much God blesses you, when you remember him, say, God, it is all about you, you deserve all the praise, you deserve all the glory. I remember when I was in the Evening Standard, and everybody was celebrating me. I'm going to say, Wow, it's amazing that you made history, you became the youngest black male Anglican priest in the UK. There are times when I was like, that's great but God is the greatest at these times. I feel like, David, I need to take off some stuff just to feel free to dance and say, Lord, I praise you. Let me just take off this "caller" for a minute and say, Lord, I give you all the glory, all the praise. I worship you. I give you all the honour, all the glory, all the worship, I praise your holy name. I lift you and give you all the glory because deep down in our hearts, we know that it's all about Him. It's all about Him, regardless of what we do, what we achieve and how far we go in life. It is all about focusing on our saviour and saying, God, thank you for the blessings. Thank you for the opportunities. Thank you for the platforms, I just want to give you all the praise and all the glory. I never want to be too high-headed to bow my knee. I never want to be too high to stop worshipping. I never want to be too high in my achievements to forget to glorify you. David was an amazing man, he did so many things. He wrote so many of the Psalms we use today.

Anyone Can Fall

David had a season and a time when he had issues in his life. Looking at David, he came to a point where he was the king of the whole of Israel. He was ruling, people went out to war for him, and his fighting days came to an end or a brief moment of pause. He was under the rooftop looking down at the kingdom and he saw somebody bathing. Despite being told she was already taken, you have so many wives, and she has a husband, he took an interest in a woman he saw bathing.

David is so passionate about God, someone who loves God so much; who has seen God deliver him from a bear, a lion, and a giant.

Someone who believes God blessed him with riches, a palace and the whole throne of Israel, you will think that he will say, she's spoken for. She's in a relationship, she's married, let me let her be. Instead, he summoned her to come to his courtyard, into his room, and he did the unthinkable: he laid with her and made love to her.

I'm thinking, oh my goodness! How can he do this? A man of God, how will it sound that he rape? I remember people were singing songs about him saying, Saul had killed his 1000s but David his 10s of 1000s. He's the same one that danced before the Ark of the Covenant. I was like, God! I'm representing you. I want to be your spokesperson. Nowadays, we speak about

15

his prophecies, about the coming Messiah, and how he expresses the pain and anguish that Jesus went through. We will think how can he do this? How can such a man of God at his level commit such an act: the sin of adultery? David? One thing I took from this is that everybody is human. Everyone stumbles occasionally. People whom we put on pedestals breathe the same air that you breathe. A lot of people get caught up in men and women of God. They're great, gifted and anointed. They're called by God but they have low moments. They have times of discrepancies in their character. They have character flaws, moments of weakness, and moments where they fail. But, the same blood of Jesus that is available for you is available for them also. Sometimes you might think, I thought they were holding the Bible, they should know that such a thing is not permitted. How dare she commit this atrocity? How dare he? They should be stoned but give them grace. Pray for the leaders. Pray for people that you know have made mistakes, that have slipped up, that have fallen. Pray for them. Cover them in prayer and love. If you're just like David, when you love God, you express your whole life for him by dancing. Maybe you are in the praise team, maybe you're running a church, or maybe you are leading the Bible study. It's just you and two old ladies and you made a mistake. Don't beat yourself up. Focus on the opinion of God. Yeah, people are going to talk. Yeah, people are going to say you should never speak again. Yeah, people might say you should never sing again, you messed up, you fell in such a big way but look up to the opinion of God who is just and able to forgive you of all your unrighteousness. Some people may never call you again. Some people might write you off for life. But, as long as God says this one has spoken to me, this one has repented, this one has bowed the knee, yes, they fell but they can get back up again. Get back up again. It doesn't matter if they're talking about you, push in God. There's nowhere else to run to. Don't turn back now. There's still more for you to do. Push in God, arise, man of God. Arise, woman of God. Keep pushing, keep praying. Don't stop, keep going forward in God. His opinion and His opinion alone is the one that counts and is the one that's going to count on the Day of Judgment. Just focus on Him.

God is not a man. If you don't turn up for their birthday party, then they block you. You don't go to their little shindig and their Christmas too, and they stop responding to you on WhatsApp. People get offended sometimes if it is blank but God is loving and His mercy endures forever. Yes, we have to live right. Yes, we have to do the right thing. Yes, we have to stand for righteousness and fight against sin but

Jesus died on the cross, for the time that we fall short, for the time that we mess up like David, for the times that we fail and fall flat on our faces. Whether it is a big sin or a small sin, whatever kind of sin, He's able to forgive you.

My Story

I remember when I was a youth preacher before I became a priest, I fell into sin: I had a child out of wedlock and so many people ripped me off. I went home in tears. I said, God, I'm done with being a Christian. I don't understand but you know more. Everybody is calling me fake, and a hypocrite. I'm going back to the world and just be a sinner, I know how to do that. That night, I had a dream. In the dream, Jesus came to me and he said, you're right, David. I was like *you're right Jesus* and then I punched him in the face. Then I was like, Oh my god, I'm so sorry, I'm so sorry. He was like, it's okay. It's okay. Then I punched him in the face again. I was like,

I'm so sorry Jesus. Oh my god, I can't believe I punch Jesus in the face. He's like, it's okay. It's all right. I punched him again in the face and was like, oh my God, I'm so sorry Jesus. I'm so sorry. He was like, David, don't worry about it. I punched him in the face again and was like, oh my God, I'm so sorry. I'm so sorry. He's like, David, don't worry about it. This happened about nine times in the dream. On the ninth time, his nose started bleeding and I started crying in the dream saying, I'm so sorry. He said, don't worry David, *I accept your sorries more than your punches.* When I woke up from that dream, I was ecstatic. I went back to the church where I was rejected, I was praising, I was dancing and

I was shouting unto the Lord. Some people came to me and said, Hey, how come this guy is so excited? Is he not the one that did something bad the other day? Let's go and investigate. No, Jesus came to me in the dream, He said I've been forgiven. He said I'd been set free. He said He loves me, hugged me, and said, don't worry, David, *I accept your sorries more than your punches.*

I realized that my being a Christian and committing fornication was like a punch to the face of Jesus. Me living that double life but every time I said sorry, I meant it. From my heart, every time I repented, I sincerely meant it and the fact that His nose started bleeding because of my punches, His blood was shed on the cross, because of our sin, His blood had to be shed, because of the things that we did.

The whole dream was like the gospel message in a language that I could understand. I told them about the dream. I told them the interpretation and they said to me, "no, David, that's quite silly. It's just your subconscious mind trying to develop a reason so that you can continue your bad behaviour. How dare you? It's just ridiculous. It doesn't make sense." This is what they said to me, they said, "if you know you're going to sin again tomorrow, there's no point repenting. I went home discouraged, and thinking, maybe it was just my subconscious mind. There's no point if I know I'm going to sin again tomorrow. What's the point in me even repenting? What is the point? I might as well just live my own life. If I ended up going to hell, then so be it.

Then the Holy Spirit spoke to me and He said, "David, that's quite silly." I was like, what do you mean? If I know I'm going to mess up tomorrow there's no point in me repenting and "Mr Man" said, that's quite silly. He said, "no one wakes up in the morning and says, I'm not going to have a shower because I'm going to get sweaty again tomorrow."

He said, "you have a shower every single day to stay fresh before people. When you confess and repent of your sins every day, that's how you stay fresh before me." I was like, hey, that's when I knew that when God speaks to you about certain things, you can't just make it up by yourself, and in your mind. You just know that you know, in your inner man. When He dropped that in my spirit, I was like, do you know what, I am not going to give up on my faith and I'm not going to give up on my assignment. I'm going to keep pushing in whatever God is telling me to do. I'm not perfect, but He is perfect and I'm going to walk with Him until I see Him and become perfect. I kept pushing.

Thank God today, I am married, and I'm still pushing in God.

Keep Your Focus on God

There are times when I've fallen short and made mistakes but after that conversation with the Holy Spirit, when I focused on God's opinion, I was able to keep going and keep pushing and also inspire people to follow God. I'm not saying that God has given you a license to do what you want to do and then repent later. I'm saying, keep pushing and keep trying to live right.

Keep fighting those sins, those desires that go against God's word, keep fighting it, keep pushing, and keep pushing and God will help you day by day to get better and better. I might not be where I want to be but I'm not where I used to be. I was a whole lot worse than I am now. That's because I kept pushing and focusing on God's opinion.

What is God saying? What is He saying in His words? What is He saying to me? Not what people over there are, people over here and people in the world are saying. What is God saying about you? He says I can use you. As long as you're still alive and breathing, I can use you. I can talk with you. I can build a relationship with you. That's all God is saying, the blood of Jesus and the grace that covers everybody else's sin can cover yours as well and God can use you to do great things and to achieve amazing things in this world. Build your relationship with him. Focus on His opinion, and His alone. Make that priority in your life, in your heart, in your mind and say to God, whatever you think, I want to align my opinion with yours. It's not about other people's opinions. It's not even about your own opinion on some set of matters but what does God think? Focus on His opinion.

Printed in Great Britain
by Amazon

Guide Your Gut

5 Simple Steps to Heal Your Microbiome and Improve

Symptoms of Crohn's, Ulcerative Colitis, and IBS

By

Kristen Fincham,

PharmD, MS, BCGP

Text Copyright ©Kristen Fincham, PharmD, MS, BCGP

ISBN: 13: 979-8-9902527-1-4

Legal & Disclaimer

Table of Contents

The Gut is The Centerpiece of our Health.

Are you putting your life on hold because you're in fear of a digestive flare up with no bathroom in sight? Or do you have to cancel events because you're lying in the fetal position from digestive pain? Maybe you feel pretty good, but you're just looking for that last puzzle piece to finally resolve your symptoms to start feeling amazing. It took me over 10 years to improve my symptoms. I'll improve yours in less than 90 days.

If you're seeking help from this book, you're likely in a dark place right feeling like you have no way out. You might be afraid to leave the house, afraid to meet new people, or afraid to do things you once loved. Work meetings might overwhelm you with anxiety because you might have to abruptly leave to use the bathroom. You might be exhausted from constant pain. You might be scared of having to deal with this for the rest of your life. You are not alone. I was there with you for many years. Millions of others are experiencing your same symptoms right now and feeling exhausted and scared that they will never get better. You can get better! And you have the power to heal yourself. You don't need to give your money to pharmaceutical companies to shove another worthless pill down your throat. You need to take the time to care for your body and heal. That's what I will show you how to do in the pages ahead.

If you complete this 90 day journey and restore your gut, you can start living your life again. I've helped countless patients restore their vitality and feel better than they've ever felt, even in their 20's. I helped a grandmother who was too afraid to babysit her new grandson for fear she may be in the bathroom too long and something terrible would happen to him. I've helped a runner get back into marathons after fear of running with no bathroom every mile. I've helped regular people get back into normal everyday life activities like dating, long car rides, and sporting events without living in fear of a flare up. Take control of your health and stop living in pain.

Why This Process Works

This process doesn't address one aspect of health, or give you one magic pill that will cure your gut, or one magic diet that will fix you. This journey will focus on my five step process that I call the Five Pillars of Gut Health, not just food or medication. And what a coincidence that the Five Pillars of Gut Health also relate to our overall health. Most books that "heal your gut" focus on a single aspect of your diet, often leaving you eating empty carbohydrates or a strict diet that isn't sustainable and actually diminishing your health.

Here, we focus on your body as a whole and bring you back to a place of balance where you can digest whole, healthy foods without pain. After going through the gut restoration journey, you will be on a path to overall wellness, leading to less gastrointestinal (GI) distress, more energy, and less risk for disease.

I consider myself a very anti-drug pharmacist. Many drugs have their place, but most of America is overmedicated. Our healthcare system likes to cover up problems with symptom-relieving medication, rather than fix the root of the problem. My goal is to improve your symptoms without prescription medications by healing the damage and getting the body back into balance.

You can choose to complete this journey on your own, or with me. I offer private sessions if you have specific questions or personal roadblocks. Visit my website to find out more at www.MedFreePharmD.com.

Chapter 1: Introduction

My qualifications, my journey and my vision for you

My Qualifications

Welcome to my guide to restoring your gut. Before we get started, I want to give you a little background on my qualifications and my own journey to healing my gut. I have my doctorate in pharmacology from USC (Fight On), a masters in Health Care Decision Analysis from USC, and a bachelors in Food Science Technology from Oregon State (Go Beavs). I also have a board specialty certification in geriatric pharmacy which means I have in depth insight on how the body changes as we get older and how we can ease these changes with some personal TLC. I got all these degrees to go to the pharmacy and count pills by fives…. Kidding. I know you think that's all pharmacists do, but we actually do know a few things too. We have a doctorate. So, we must have learned something after all those years. My job as a clinical pharmacist is to understand the ins and outs of human physiology, how substances (such as drugs, food, or chemicals) affect the body, how the body affects these substances, and how multiple substances within the body affect each other.

This knowledge helps me understand the body as a whole and how the smallest changes can damage our body. My education in food science combined with my understanding of physiology give me a unique perspective on how the modern-day diet and food processing is interacting with the human body and, well, killing us. In my career as a pharmacist, I've discovered that the gut is the centerpiece of our health. A damaged gut can lead to pain, discomfort, and disease. A healed gut can improve all aspects of health. After meeting with me and following my process, my patients have lessened their medications, had significant improvement in their symptoms, some became completely symptom free and even stated they feel better than they ever have! I wrote this book to reach more people and show them they have the power to heal themselves.

My Journey

My problems started when I was 18 years old. I lost my only sibling two weeks before my high school graduation. Six weeks later I had to move out of state, start training for division I collegiate soccer, and adjust to the rigors of college academics. This was slightly traumatic. I was exhausted, sad, depressed, angry, and alone. Soccer used to be my outlet, but my body was so exhausted from grief that it took every ounce of energy and strength to make it through a practice and I hated every second of it. Not to mention I was 1,000 miles away from home, didn't know anyone, and transitioning into collegiate athlete life. I was playing the worst I had ever played in my life, I was more exhausted than I had ever been in my life, I was angrier than I had ever been in my life, and more depressed than I had ever been in my life.

Luckily I had wonderful parents, coaches and teammates who were extremely understanding of my situation and my terrible performance on the field. Thanks to them I made it through that first year in a depressed haze, but I made it. I got to go home and be with my parents and friends for the summer and reset. I started my second year off feeling much better. I could make it through more than one day without crying, I started to play better, I was in the starting lineup in many games and feeling good. I was just beginning to feel like myself again, remembering what it was to laugh and not constantly feel like I was in darkness. It was feeling like things would be okay.

Then everything changed. I tore my ACL (again) and had my fourth knee surgery. A few months after the surgery, I started feeling this overwhelming sense of fatigue to the point that I was sleeping over 14 hours at night, napping during the day and it took every ounce of willpower to work out. I felt brain fog and couldn't remember things from class. I started having serious urgency when needing to use the bathroom. The feeling would come on suddenly. If I didn't make it to the bathroom in less than five minutes then I wasn't making it.

The first time I realized the urgency was a serious problem, I was at Crystal Cove State Park with my parents and my now married friends, Blake and Michele. For those of you who haven't been there, this is a beautiful state beach in California. The problem for me that day was that the bathrooms are up a very steep hill and not close by. We were having a great time hanging out in the sun in our bathing suits and drinking our ice cold Coors Lights. The mountains were blue. Suddenly, I realized I needed to go to the bathroom. Immediately! I started walking up the hill, but that wasn't fast enough. I started running, but the jostling was making the pain worse. I settled for a power walk while holding everything in with all my might. Right when I could see the bathrooms, when I was so close, just a swimming pool's length away, I didn't make it. I'm at the beach in a bathing suit, remember. This was unfortunate. Luckily the bathroom was empty and I was able to deal with the situation.

When I made it back to the beach my family and friends were laughing and having a great time. They jokingly asked if I made it, thinking, "of course she made it." And I shook my head and said, "no I didn't." Blake said, "Kristen, that is what we call an SSS, a Sudden Sh*t Syndrome." Luckily we are the type of people that can laugh about this and I still laugh about it to this day. The term SSS has stuck with my family for over 13 years now and has been passed on to many others. After that, I had a few more incidents and many close calls. None quite as public as that one. This was the day I realized my fatigue and my SSS's meant something is wrong here.

From that point on I went to countless doctors. I was tested for everything from celiac disease to cancer. I had CT scans, a colonoscopy, an endoscopy and countless other tests. They looked at my diet, sleep, and exercise habits. As a division I collegiate athlete, I was the picture of health. Every doctor gave me the same answer: nothing is wrong with you. Then they would relate it back to the stress and depression related to my brother's death and say my issues are due to that. Then they would write me a prescription for an antidepressant and tell me to keep Pepto Bismol on hand. The problem was, this all started at a time in my life when I was feeling better and coming out of depression.

A couple years went by with this pattern of suffering and no solutions. At this point, I was getting my doctorate in pharmacology and I knew better than to experiment with antidepressants when I wasn't depressed. Although I would (and always will) feel a deep sadness related to the loss of my brother, it wasn't overtaking me as it had the previous years. The fatigue was a different type of feeling than before. Where did this fecal urgency come from? Where did these debilitating stomach pains come from? I couldn't accept the answer that nothing was wrong with me. There *was* something wrong with me.

By my second year of pharmacy school I was taking over the counter painkillers so often for my stomach pain that I was getting kidney stones. Things were getting worse. Panic would set in if my train to school was late because I might not make it to the bathroom. Activities like snowboarding became difficult because I had to stop every couple runs to use the bathroom. One time, I sobbed in a gas station because their bathroom was out of order and people definitely thought I was a crazy person. I won't even get into the floating the river event where the porta potty was full when I was first dating my husband. My entire life revolved around my GI tract.

After a year of seeing a certain doctor with no diagnosis, he said to me that he discovered he had a sensitivity to wheat later in life and maybe it's a food sensitivity. A food sensitivity? Here I am thinking I have intestinal cancer and I could have something as simple as a food sensitivity? I had been seeing this doctor and multiple others for over a year and no one thought to mention this to me? I was annoyed.

Since every doctor's answer for why I was in the fetal position with stomach pain was because I was stressed and depressed, I left the doctors' offices behind. I started reading books, researching stomach problems and finding out everything I could about urgency and stomach pain.

This started me down the path of over eight different elimination diets that took me years to complete, experimenting with different supplements, and examining every aspect of health I could. Books that preached they would heal me would only address one or two factors of gut health and I'd be left feeling the same. Other books cut out certain healthy foods, but left in high-carb processed food that had me feeling sluggish and exhausted.

After more than 10 years of learning and experimentation, I finally came up with my own recipe for success and reached a point in my life where I'm not running to the bathroom or constipated or having debilitating stomach pain, I have clear skin, and I have more energy than I had in my 20's and even my teens. I have also helped patients just like you reach a point of relief in as little as 90 days. Many start to have some symptom relief in just two weeks.

My Vision for You

Healing your gut doesn't have to be as complicated as it was for me. My knowledge of pharmacology, physiology and food science have come together to help me understand how the food we eat and the processing of that food affect our entire picture of health. Those 10 years of my personal journey plus the last six years helping patients as a pharmacist have shown me that gut health is the centerpiece of our overall wellness and vitality. Restoring our gut comes down to five simple steps, or as I call them, pillars: sleep, diet, supplements, stress management and exercise. And unlike me, this process will only take you 90 days, not 10 years.

You're 90 days away from living your life!

Chapter 2: How to Use This Guide

Let's talk about who this is for and how to go through this guide successfully

Who is This For?

This book is for people suffering from any number of digestive issues. Symptoms can include: gas, bloating, heartburn, diarrhea, urgency, constipation, and many others. This can be used by patients with a diagnosis such as ulcerative colitis, Crohn's, or irritable bowel syndrome (IBS). It can also be used by people like me who have been told nothing is wrong with you, feel you are very healthy, but continue to have digestive issues. Many people with gut issues also suffer from skin problems, fatigue, and brain fog. Don't be surprised when your gut isn't the only thing that starts to feel better after this process.

As I stated earlier, I consider myself a very anti-drug pharmacist. Many drugs have their place, but most Americans are over medicated. Many patients with GI issues are given a pill that just covers up their symptoms and lessens the pain. None of these medications address the root of the problem. Many of these medications could be making the problem worse. Leading to more medications and on and on the cycle goes.

If you haven't seen your doctor about these issues, I encourage you to do so. **Check in with your doctor before making any changes involved in this book.** If you are taking medications, also check in with your pharmacist.

The Overview

This book is meant to be a guide to healing that gets to the point. I don't bombard you with charts, studies, and in-depth information. I give you enough background to help you understand the purpose of each step, then we dive into the process. If you want to go deeper into the research, I provide references. My own process took over 10 years of trial and error to feel better and countless books and research articles. I've taken what I've learned and created a process that will have you feeling better in 90 days, not 10 years. And you don't have to read the whole library to figure it out. This should be a quick read so you can get going on improving your health rather than sitting and reading pages and pages of research. I've already done the research for you.

The Process

This book is broken down into three sections: Restore, Rebuild, and Revitalize. These three sections encompass my five step process - The Five Pillars of Health: Sleep, Diet, Supplements, Movement, and Stress Management. Each section is 30 days, the overall journey is 90 days. I provide background information first, then explain the process step by step. You don't necessarily have to complete all of these steps over 90 days. If you are more of a baby step kind of person, then go at your own speed. If you want to increase the number of days of each section, go for it. However, do not shorten the number of days. For example, if you want to take the recommended supplements for longer than 30 days, great! But don't take them for less than 30 days.

This requires work on your side. The more committed you are to the process, the greater transformation you will see. Though this journey will present challenges for you, I know you can do it. I did it and so did so many other patients of mine. If you need extra support or personal modifications for your situation, book a private appointment with me on my website and I can be with you every step of the way. Or let a friend know you are doing this so you have someone to be accountable to.

Some things in this book will involve what I call "forever changes" and some will be temporary. Forever changes are things you should incorporate into your lifestyle forever. The forever changes are good for your overall health as well as gut health. The temporary changes allow time for healing and identifying your personal triggers. Incorporating these temporary changes help us resolve your symptoms faster.

First things first: you need a journal. I call this the Food and Symptom Journal, FSJ for short. I highly recommend using my *Guide Your Gut Companion: A 90 Day Food and Symptom Journal*. You can download it from my website at http://www.medfreepharmd.com/fsj. My FSJ (as we will call it from now on) is set up to follow along with each section of the book. This will keep you on track every day with each pillar, each change, and allow you space to record your symptoms. It will be your companion through this journey. You can also use your own journal. It doesn't matter as long as you can have a journal with you every day.

Have your journal? Great. Let's make our intentions clear.

1. Write down your symptoms.

2. How are these affecting your life?

3. What is motivating you to seek help and make a change?

4. Where do you hope your symptoms will be 30 days from now?

5. Where do you hope your symptoms will be 60 days from now?

6. Where do you hope they will be at the end of this journey?

7. What are your weaknesses when it comes to making changes?

8. What is your plan to overcome these weaknesses?

9. Write down your goals for the next 90 days and how you will stick to them.

Let's get started! Below, you will find the schedule of the overall journey to give you an idea of where we're headed.

Day 1	Day 2	Day 3	Day 4	Day 5	Day 6	Day 7
Sleep	Sleep	Sleep	Sleep	Sleep	Sleep	Sleep
Hydrate	Hydrate	Hydrate	Hydrate	Hydrate	Hydrate	Hydrate
Eliminate poisons and irritants	Eliminate poisons and irritants	Eliminate poisons and irritants	Eliminate poisons and irritants	Eliminate poisons and irritants	Eliminate poisons and irritants	Eliminate poisons and irritants

Day 8	Day 9	Day 10	Day 11	Day 12	Day 13	Day 14
Sleep	Sleep	Sleep	Sleep	Sleep	Sleep	Sleep
Hydrate	Hydrate	Hydrate	Hydrate	Hydrate	Hydrate	Hydrate
Eliminate poisons and irritants	Eliminate poisons and irritants	Eliminate poisons and irritants	Eliminate poisons and irritants	Eliminate poisons and irritants	Eliminate poisons and irritants	Eliminate poisons and irritants

Day 15	Day 16	Day 17	Day 18	Day 19	Day 20	Day 21
Sleep	Sleep	Sleep	Sleep	Sleep	Sleep	Sleep
Hydrate	Hydrate	Hydrate	Hydrate	Hydrate	Hydrate	Hydrate
Add one irritant back in			Add one irritant back in			Add one irritant back in

Day 22	Day 23	Day 24	Day 25	Day 26	Day 27	Day 28
Sleep	Sleep	Sleep	Sleep	Sleep	Sleep	Sleep
Hydrate	Hydrate	Hydrate	Hydrate	Hydrate	Hydrate	Hydrate
		Add one irritant back in			Add one irritant back in	

Day 29	Day 30	Day 31	Day 32	Day 33	Day 34	Day 35
Sleep	Sleep					
Hydrate	Hydrate	Add Collagen				Add L-Glutamine
	Add one irritant back in					

Day 36	Day 37	Day 38	Day 39	Day 40	Day 41	Day 42
				Add Fish Oil		

Day 43	Day 44	Day 45	Day 46	Day 47	Day 48	Day 49
		Add Reishi				

Day 50	Day 51	Day 52	Day 53	Day 54	Day 55	Day 56
Add Probiotics					Add Fiber	

Day 57	Day 58	Day 59	Day 60	Day 61	Day 62	Day 63
				Exercise Meditate Chosen fasting plan	Exercise Meditate Chosen fasting plan	Exercise Meditate Chosen fasting plan

Day 64	Day 65	Day 66	Day 67	Day 68	Day 69	Day 70
Exercise Meditate Chosen fasting plan	Exercise Meditate Chosen fasting plan	Exercise Meditate Chosen fasting plan	Exercise Meditate Chosen fasting plan	Exercise Meditate Chosen fasting plan	Exercise Meditate Chosen fasting plan	Exercise Meditate Chosen fasting plan

Day 71	Day 72	Day 73	Day 74	Day 75	Day 76	Day 77
Exercise Meditate Chosen fasting plan	Exercise Meditate Chosen fasting plan	Exercise Meditate Chosen fasting plan	Exercise Meditate Chosen fasting plan	Exercise Meditate Chosen fasting plan	Exercise Meditate Chosen fasting plan	Exercise Meditate Chosen fasting plan

Day 78	Day 79	Day 80	Day 81	Day 82	Day 83	Day 84
Exercise	Exercise	Exercise	Exercise	Exercise	Exercise	Exercise
Meditate	Meditate	Meditate	Meditate	Meditate	Meditate	Meditate
Chosen fasting plan	Chosen fasting plan	Chosen fasting plan	Chosen fasting plan	Chosen fasting plan	Chosen fasting plan	Chosen fasting plan
Day 85	Day 86	Day 87	Day 88	Day 89	Day 90	DONE!!!
Exercise	Exercise	Exercise	Exercise	Exercise	Exercise	You made it!
Meditate	Meditate	Meditate	Meditate	Meditate	Meditate	
Chosen fasting plan	Chosen fasting plan	Chosen fasting plan	Chosen fasting plan	Chosen fasting plan	Chosen fasting plan	

Chapter 3: What is Gut Health?

What is the gut?

Before we dive straight in and fix your need to sprint to the bathroom every day, we need to understand what is going on inside your body. Let's discuss what your gut really is. Gut health is such a buzz word these days. But what does it mean? There is so much to say about all the functions of the gut because it is the centerpiece of our health. I will just give you a brief summary here. Your "gut" or your gastrointestinal system starts at your mouth, includes your stomach, intestines, colon and rectum. The main job of your gastrointestinal tract is to breakdown food and absorb nutrients. As more research comes out, we are finding the gut is responsible for more than just processing food. Your gut health affects mood, inflammation, disease progression, immune function, weight, and so much more.

The intestinal barrier is made up of multiple complex layers and physiological processes. We have the microbial barrier which is made up of trillions of microorganisms. We will go in depth on the microbial layer and microbiome later in the chapter. You have gut mucus that accumulates between the intestinal lumen and the brush border of the enterocytes. The mucus layer protects the epithelial cells, acts as a transport medium for cells, and provides a habitat for microorganisms. The functional barrier contains gastric acid, biliary secretions, and pancreatic secretions to help process food. The epithelial layer contains enterocytes and tight junctions. The enterocytes are cells that line the intestinal epithelium. These cells are the physical barrier between what you bring into your intestines and the rest of your body. These cells absorb nutrients, prevent pathogen invasion, and interact with immune cells to keep your body healthy. The tight junctions are structures between the cells which seal off the gaps and regulate the entrance of ions, molecules, and other cells. The intestines also contain the immunological barrier. Over 70% of your immune system resides in your gut through a combination of pathogen fighting cells and barriers preventing pathogens from entering the body. Other layers I will quickly mention include the gut vascular barrier and the liver barrier. As you can see, the gut is an extremely intricate system that both fuels you through nutrients from your food and protects you from pathogens and toxins.

What is Going on in <u>Your</u> Gut?

In short, your gut is damaged if you're seeking help from this book. Now, I'm making the assumption here that you have visited your doctor and been tested for an array of diseases and left with no answers and told either nothing is wrong or you have Crohn's, Ulcerative Colitis, or IBS. So, if you haven't seen your doctor, please do so and make sure you don't have something going on. Don't implement any changes in this book until you see your doctor. For everyone else keep reading.

When your gut is giving you all these painful symptoms it's because the intricate system discussed above is damaged. That damage is likely not one little thing, but a collection of problems that has grown over a period of time and brought you to the place of suffering you're in now. The damage includes, but is not limited to the following: physical damage of the epithelial layers that we talked about above and a microbiome that has more harmful bacteria than helpful bacteria. The term leaky gut is thrown around a lot as well. Remember the tight junctions I mentioned above? These tight junctions are thought to be damaged and allow large molecules and pathogens to pass through in individuals with leaky gut. How did this damage happen to you? A combination of factors that include: lack of sleep, toxic food additives, chronic stress, trauma (physical or emotional), and lack of physical activity. American culture has become very sedentary, very high stress, and very reliant on convenience leading to unhealthy amounts of processed food consumption. You may have all these factors at play or one thing taking the lead role. Either way, the symptoms you're experiencing are your body telling you there is damage.

What is the microbiome?

Your gut doesn't do its job all alone. It gets by with a little help from its friends. You know, like that Beatles song. Microorganisms such as bacteria, fungi, and viruses make up what we call the microbiome. You have more bacteria cells in your body than you do your own cells. So, let's just say these little tiny friends are pretty important in your overall health. And these little friends also have foes. When your microbiome is taken over by detrimental microorganisms (the foes) it can destroy your system in more ways than one. The makeup of your microbiome can make or break your health. I will refer to your microbiome often in this book. For our purposes, it will mean the microorganisms in your digestive tract.

When your microbiome is unbalanced (more foes than friends), your system is out of balance. Dysbiosis, as we call it, can lead to problems all over the body. This is becoming a very common issue in the United States. Why? The modern-day diet is far removed from what our ancestors ate. According to the CDC, the average American consumes 60% of their daily food as processed food. Other sources estimate it's closer to 90%. The problem is much worse in America as opposed to other countries for several reasons. For one, we allow many more additives in our food than other countries. These additives damage our "friends" in our microbiome. Another reason is, we are always on the go and convenience is everything to us. Where does this lead us? To eating processed foods via meal replacement bars, packaged foods, prepared foods, and fast food. Unlike some other countries where preparing meals and eating them with family and extended family is the norm, our norm is hurry, hurry, hurry, go, go, go convenience is key. This convenience lifestyle full of food additives is leading to disease, weight gain, inflammation, and even mental health disorders.

Another key player in an unbalanced microbiome is the use of antibiotics. Antibiotics are a wonderful life-saving tool in medicine. However, they were being passed out like candy for quite a while for every little cold and sniffle. Every time a course of antibiotics is taken, it kills the bacteria responsible for your infection, but it also completely wipes out your beneficial microbes as well. If you've taken a few courses of antibiotics in your life then you probably have a very unbalanced microbiome in your gut. Unfortunately, we're also finding antibiotics in our food. The beef, poultry, pork, dairy, and farmed fish industries are allowed to give their animals antibiotics. We then consume these antibiotics when we eat these foods. Make sure to read your labels to know where your animal products are coming from and whether they were given antibiotics. Don't get me wrong, antibiotics have their place in medicine! They just need to be used sparingly to avoid dysbiosis.

Dysbiosis can lead to an array of health problems. Unhealthy weight gain can be a product of dysbiosis. A 2012 study published in Nature discovered the gut microbiota of obese people was very different from thin people. When the microbiota of obese people was transplanted into germ-free mice, fat deposition increased, indicating a direct correlation between the makeup of gut bacteria and metabolism. Unhealthy bacteria can produce toxins making it difficult to lose weight. They create unhealthy cravings for foods that fuel these bacteria, but destroy your health. Eventually this creates a never-ending cycle of cravings, toxins, and weight gain. Getting your gut into balance can end this cycle and lead to weight loss with very little effort.

One of the most important connections is the gut brain connection. More research is finding that distress in the digestive tract sends signals to the brain that increase risk of depression and anxiety. Individuals with functional bowel problems have a higher rate of depression. Many refer to the gut as a "second brain." If our second brain is out of balance, our brain will receive the wrong signals, leading to mood, anxiety, and mental health issues.

Inflammation is another huge buzz word topic in health. Inflammation with no clear cause is due to putting poison in our body. It's as simple as that. If you poison your digestive tract with toxic substances, you damage your gut lining, you kill off your microorganism friends, and you feed the microorganism foes. The foes create toxic metabolites that are absorbed leading to alarm signals causing your body to release inflammatory compounds. Chronic inflammation can damage every organ and lead to an array of diseases.

An unbalanced microbiome also negatively affects your immune system. Are you constantly getting sick in addition to all your digestive issues? It's probably because over 70% of your immune system exists in your gut. Your immune system is interacting with all the microorganisms in your gut. When you have a healthy, balanced microbiome, your immune system is able to focus on the real intruders and keep you healthy. If you're fueling the foes in your microbiome, then your immune system is under distress, overworked and overtired. Research has shown that your microbiome make-up can affect your response to certain medical treatments. Studies published in Cell Host & Microbe in 2019 revealed that the gut microbiota may even affect how well cancer immunotherapy works.

Of course, the main reason you're here is your digestive issues. Whether that be Crohn's, Ulcerative Colitis, IBS, or just general, undiagnosed digestive problems, the microbiome is the source of the problem. An unbalanced microbiome leads to all of the painful symptoms: heartburn, urgency, incontinence, damaged gut lining, diarrhea, constipation, bloating, indigestion, pain, and on and on the list goes. Why? Because your microbiome plays a major role in breaking down your food. Microbes break down complex carbohydrates and fiber. They also contain enzymes necessary to produce certain vitamins. Additionally, they help breakdown bile to help your body reabsorb and recycle. When your microbes aren't doing these things, it leads to problematic digestion. Our goal here is to heal your microbiome, create more microorganism friends than foes, heal the physical damage in your gastrointestinal tract, and improve your symptoms, your health, and your life.

Training Your Microbiome

All steps in this book have to do with training your microbiome, which will also help to heal the physical damage in your intestinal epithelium. What I mean by this is you will be undertaking steps to create more "friends" in your GI tract than "foes." Your microbiome is made up of different colonies of microbes. These microbes send signals to your brain based on their needs. These signals include telling your brain what to eat. The larger the colony is, the more power it has over your brain. If you have a very large colony of sugar-craving bacteria, then you likely have very strong sugar cravings. And every time you "feed the craving" you are quite literally feeding these microbes allowing the colony to thrive and even push out beneficial bacteria.

The ideal microbiome is diverse and of course, beneficial. Your microbiome can make or break your health.

A healthy microbiome helps you break down foods, absorb important nutrients, and energize your cells. A damaged microbiome causes you to crave unhealthy foods, prevents appropriate breakdown of nutrients, prevents absorption of nutrients, creates damage to your GI lining, causes inflammation that spreads through the entire body, and leads to all these symptoms that has led you to this book: diarrhea, constipation, urgency, heartburn, cramping, pain, etc.

One strain of bacteria I will share with you is *Faecalibacterium prausnitzii*. This strain fights for the good guys, he's our friend. This bacteria is responsible for breaking down fiber and producing butyrate. Butyrate has many benefits to the body. For one, it is a major fuel source for your colonocytes. These are the epithelial cells in the lining of your colon. Butyrate modulates the tight junctions in your intestines, promotes mucus production, and protects your epithelial barrier. Other benefits include insulin sensitivity, weight control, anti-inflammatory properties, and a range of immune system benefits. It's kind of an important one if you can't tell. Studies have shown that low levels of *F. prausnitzii* are associated with major digestive issues including IBS, celiac disease, constipation, Crohn's, and Ulcerative Colitis. Low levels are also associated with type 2 diabetes, colorectal cancer and psoriasis. This is just one strain! Imagine the damage that can be caused when your entire microbiome is out whack if this one tiny strain can be associated with so much good and low levels with so much damage. So, what probiotic am I going to tell you to go buy right now to stuff yourself full of *F. prausnitzii*? Well, unfortunately this little guy is extremely oxygen sensitive and will die when exposed to air, meaning you can't take this in supplement form. You have to care for your microbiome, heal it, and feed it the appropriate foods to increase your levels of *F. prausnitzii*. Luckily, we're going to do that in this book.

As you go through this book, and really the rest of your life, you should start to think about your microbiome as your internal garden. Your intestines are your soil, your food is your fertilizer, your water is your, well, water, and your processed foods are like dumping Roundup all over your garden. You need to cultivate your microbiome to grow the beneficial colonies and shrink the negative colonies. Strive to eat the foods that benefit your garden, and strive to eliminate the foods that destroy your garden.

This book will be a kickstart to growing your beneficial microbiome. If you follow the principles here, you will be on your way to cultivating a microbiome which breaks down your nutrients appropriately, helps you absorb disease

41

fighting nutrients, fills you with energy, maintains a healthy immune system, and the reason you're all here, reduces and even eliminates your painful digestion.

The Importance of the Microbiome Outside the GI Tract

We just discussed the microbiome in your GI tract, but did you know you have microbes all over your body that affect your health? Improving your gut microbiome can help improve the other microbiomes on and in your body.

Skin Microbiome: The skin microbiome, made up of different bacteria, fungi, and viruses, is essential for preserving the skin's pH balance, regulating immune responses, and shielding the skin from infections. Acne, eczema, and psoriasis have all been related to disruptions in the skin microbiome. According to a 2019 study published in Nature Communications, people with acne had very different skin microbiomes than people with clear skin. Particular bacteria, such as *Propionibacterium acnes,* which can cause inflammation and the formation of acne lesions, were shown to be more prevalent in the skin of people who were prone to acne.

Oral Microbiome: The collection of bacteria, viruses, and fungi that live in the mouth and oral cavity is known as the oral microbiome. It is essential to keep your mouth and oral cavity healthy, and it can also affect your general health. Tooth decay, periodontal disorders, and even systemic problems like diabetes and cardiovascular disease are linked to imbalances in the oral microbiome. A 2018 publication in the *Journal of Dental Research* emphasized the part the oral microbiota plays in the onset of periodontitis. The severity of periodontal disease was correlated with dysbiosis in the oral microbiome, which is defined by an overgrowth of periodontal pathogens.

Reproductive Microbiome: The importance of the microbiome of the reproductive system, notably the female vagina, in reproductive health, fertility, and pregnancy outcomes is becoming well-acknowledged. Imbalances in the vaginal microbiota can result in diseases like bacterial vaginosis and raise the possibility of unfavorable pregnancy outcomes, such as preterm birth. A 2016 study published in *Science Translational Medicine* discovered a link between the preterm birth risk and the makeup of the vaginal microbiota during pregnancy. More specifically, compared to women whose vaginal microbiome was dominated by other bacteria, those whose microbiome was dominated by *Lactobacillus* had a decreased risk of premature birth.

The microbiome is an essential component of human health which affects various physiological processes and aids in the onset and advancement of many diseases. Gaining knowledge about the makeup and functions of the microbiome has enormous potential to further therapeutic and preventive measures that enhance human health and well-being.

Why Your Medications Are Not Curing Your GI Issues

Have you gone to your doctor with this problem and all they tell you is "nothing is wrong with you" and send you on your way with a prescription? I think everyone with IBS has experienced this. I was given a lot of useless answers, everything from "you're depressed because your brother died," to "you have heartburn." Never, in any appointment did I describe any symptom related to heartburn, yet I left with a heartburn prescription. I didn't take it though. Unfortunately doctors only have about 7-15 minutes to spend with their patient. These days, their goal is making sure you're not dying when you leave. They don't have time to sit you down and explain the microbiome and create a personalized healing process for you. They have time to write you a prescription. Please don't blame your physician; they do not enjoy this reality of their job either. As a pharmacist, I've had many patients come into the pharmacy with a new prescription hopeful that this magical drug will fix them and they will finally find relief. Unfortunately, when they come back for their refill their hope is usually gone and they maybe find slight relief at the most. All these IBS medications are working in different ways to do the same thing. They are dampening your body's alarm response, and doing nothing to solve the problem.

Let's compare this to a home alarm. Home alarms are jarring and loud because they want you to wake up and know there is an intruder in your house. Now, you could just turn the alarm off and go back to bed. You got rid of the annoying sound, but you did nothing to get rid of the intruder. He's still there damaging your home and taking all your stuff. When he leaves, he will probably tell his friends that this house doesn't do anything to you if you break in. You might have another intruder soon with another annoying alarm. So then maybe you decide to just not set the alarm at night at all since it keeps going off due to these darn intruders! The damage will keep building with intruder after intruder, but hey at least you

45

don't have that annoying alarm sound going off! Would you do that? No, of course not! This is what these medications are doing. They turn off or dampen your body's alarm so you have less of the annoying symptoms. But, on the inside, all the damage is still happening. Over a period of time of dampened symptoms, but continued damage, your problem on the inside is likely getting worse.

I don't discourage any medications as a short-term crutch that helps you find relief if you are really suffering. I do discourage these as a long-term solution because they are not a solution at all. They are doing nothing to heal the damage, build your microbiome, or improve your health. If you are on a medication then use it only as a crutch. If you broke your leg, you wouldn't just take painkillers and keep walking on it. You would heal the broken bone.

If you are currently on a medication for your symptoms, please talk to your pharmacist before making changes. Let them know you are undergoing this process and ask their advice for when it is safe to discontinue the medication.

Chapter 4: Improvement, Not Perfection

As you embark on this journey, you will find challenges. The challenges really depend on where you are at with your symptoms. Some of you may have tried other solutions before, some of you might be right at the beginning. Some of you may be suffering severely, and some may just be trying to fix that last little annoying problem. Wherever you are at, challenges are part of any transformative journey, so don't feel alone. The goal here isn't perfection, it is improvement. Take note of where you are now and why you want to change. Continue to celebrate the small wins.

The diet phase is where many people struggle. I'm not telling you to do anything I don't do myself. I made some of these changes while I was working, commuting, and working on my doctorate. I continued these changes through pregnancy and being a full-time working mom of two. I know you don't have time, you're busy, you're tired, you're working, you're commuting, or sometimes you just plain don't want to. We all feel that way. A transformation takes work. And that's just that.

This is where we need to talk about non-negotiables. People who have pooped their pants in public like I did, might have very few non-negotiables. Mine pretty much went away after that experience. I was willing to do anything to get better. People whose symptoms are not quite as debilitating may have more non-negotiables. Now, your non-negotiables are completely up to you. Things I have encountered with my private clients include: not giving up coffee for 14 days, not giving up poison-filled coffee creamer, wanting to eat chocolate cake often, drinking hot chocolate every morning, using a meal delivery service, packaged snacks, soda, or their favorite meal replacement bar.

This is your transformation, not mine. I did mine. I don't run to the bathroom anymore or cry in the fetal position. Well, sometimes I cry in the fetal position, but not from digestive pain. The clients who enter this process with an open mind, willing to make changes see the greatest results. Your transformation is up to you. If you don't want to give things up you likely won't see the results you're hoping for.

But, life is about balance right! It's your choice how far you want to take your transformation. I like to remind my clients that we are only giving up certain things for 14 days. Anyone can give up anything for 14 days. Other things we give up are causing disease inside your body. Now that I have healed my IBS, I do eat a few things that I know may cause a flare up. But I rarely have one because I put the time in to heal my body and it can handle those triggers every once in a while now.

"Falling off the wagon" as we call it in my family is another big challenge. Many people start a healing journey so motivated and ready to change! They do all the checklist items and tell their friends and family how great it is and they're finally going to get better! And then they remember life. And they decided one little cheat day won't hurt. And then one turns into two. And then their job gets stressful. And then they have a kid on the way. And then they're moving. And then someone is getting married. And then they have their big vacation planned. And then a family member gets sick. And then and then and then….. There's never a time in life that is easy. And when it is, the next thing is just around the corner. Start making changes now. You may fall off the wagon here or there, but you can get right back on. What I'm trying to say is have an open mind and remember everyone's life is busy and full of surprises and obstacles. Remember, you can always come back to this. Small changes are wins too!

Making a life-changing transformation isn't about motivation. It's about discipline. You're here now because you're motivated and excited to get better. That feeling may not last. People who have the greatest successes in all areas of life don't have daily motivation and excitement, they have discipline. I don't work out every day because I get excited about it. I work out every day because I'm disciplined and I know it benefits me today as well as benefits my future self. Below are some ways to stay disciplined in this process:

1. Write out your symptoms, why they are debilitating, why you want to change.
2. Write your goals and where you want to be.
3. Prioritize the steps in this book. Some steps may be harder for you than others. Make note of that and complete the easy steps first if that works better for you.

4. Know your weaknesses. Know what you tend to give in to. Write down ways to avoid giving in to these weaknesses.
5. Change your perspective. Think about the new things you may discover if you complete all the steps in this book. Maybe you can start doing an activity again you had to stop. Maybe you can eat at restaurants again without fear. Maybe your skin problems will improve. Maybe you will stop getting sick so much. Maybe you will set a lifelong example for your kids on how to live a healthy lifestyle.
6. Forgive yourself. If you stumble, forgive yourself, move forward and try again. Remember, our goal here isn't perfection, it's improvement.

Everyone is different. You should do what works for you. Improvement over perfection is the goal. Remember to think about the microbiome living inside you and feed the microbes you want to grow and don't feed the ones you want to get rid of. The more you give into this process, the more benefits you will receive.

Chapter 5: Restore

Pillar 1: Sleep and Pillar 2: Diet

The diet phase is by far the most involved and most in-depth part of this process. Once you make it through the diet phase you will coast through the rest. We're going to start on an easier note first which is sleep.

Pillar 1: Sleep

The first major step in this book is to sleep. This is going to be so easy. You're welcome. Getting enough sleep can heal, prevent, or decrease the risk of almost every health issue on the planet. People say, "sleep when you're dead." Well, you will be dead much sooner if you don't sleep while you're alive, so I guess that saying is true. Sleep is usually the lowest priority when people get too busy. Many believe that sleep is less important than other aspects of health. This is not true at all, and might possibly be the most important pillar of this book. Sleep is an extremely active process. Think of it as the nightly janitor of your mind and body. Sleep is the time that your body repairs, restores, and refuels your system, including your gut. I call it my cleaning cycle. On nights where my sleep is severely shortened, such as getting up at 3:00 AM to catch a plane, I have diarrhea that next day.

I've always prioritized sleep. I'm not really sure why. Maybe my parents ingrained the importance in me. Maybe I just realized I felt awful when I didn't sleep enough. But I actually used to feel quite frustrated that I *needed* my full eight hours every night. I thought that I must be lazy or weak. Other people could sleep less, why couldn't I? I felt absolutely terrible, foggy, and sluggish when my sleep was interrupted. I went through phases where I tried to force myself to sleep less so I could get more done in a day. During these times I felt awful. It wasn't until I read *Why We Sleep* by Mathew Walker, PhD., that I realized I wasn't lazy. Everyone needs a full seven to eight hours of sleep. Because I prioritized sleep my whole life, I realized the effects lack of sleep had on my body, whereas others didn't realize how good they could feel if they did prioritize sleep. *Why We Sleep* goes into extreme detail on the importance of sleep and it is fascinating. Sleep alone can improve symptoms or decrease risk of almost every disease we can think of. Sleeping a full seven to eight hours every night can even help you lose weight. Yes, you can get skinny while lying in bed!

To stay focused on the topic at hand, let's talk about sleep and gut health. Sleep does two main things for your gut health: improves your microbiome and helps with nutrient absorption. As we have already learned, a healthy microbiome is vital to a healthy gut. Adequate sleep has proven to maintain and flourish the healthy microbes in your gut creating an environment of optimal nutrient absorption and pain free digestion. Adequate sleep also calms the nervous system. This means your fight or flight system relaxes allowing your body to allocate that energy to your gut creating an optimal environment for digestion. A healthy microbiome and a calmed nervous system will help restore your gut and help you gain the most benefit from this process. Let your body's janitor come in every night and do it's job.

During the restore phase you will allow yourself the opportunity to sleep a full 7 to 8 hours every night. I personally do best with 8, some people feel better with 7. This might mean you have to give up a TV show or video games or extra reading each night. During this phase you will work out how to adjust your schedule to allow for 7 to 8 hours. Falling asleep on the couch while watching TV does not count. Sleep is one of the best and easiest things you can do for your health. It will improve your gut health, your overall health, focus, productivity, and decrease your risk of many diseases. If you think you are one of those people that only need four hours of sleep and you're good to go, you're probably wrong. The gene mutation that allows people to be short sleepers without any negative health effects is thought to only be present in about one out of every 4 million to 8 million people (study results vary).

A very common theme in American society is sleeping pills. I have countless patients on sleeping pills. As a pharmacist, I am strongly against them. If you are someone that takes sleeping pills, GET OFF THEM! Talk to your doctor or pharmacist first before stopping any medications. These pills are preventing your clean-out process every night and can even be adding to early Alzheimer's, dementia, psychotic episodes, and obviously GI issues.

Look at your schedule and determine what changes you need to make to give yourself the opportunity to sleep 7 to 8 hours each night. You may need to set an alarm to notify you to turn off the TV and go to bed. You may realize you can prep some things the night before while you watch TV and not have to get up so early. Maybe you're one of those people that sets five alarms and only gets up after the last alarm (and your alarm also wakes up your spouse five times). Stop doing this. Just set the last alarm and stop interrupting your sleep earlier than you need to. Studies have shown you feel better if you don't hit the snooze button and just get up. These 30 days you will trial what works best for you in order for you to get the sleep you need every night. After you figure out what works best for you, this will become a forever change. You should prioritize seven to eight hours of sleep every night.

Here comes the push back. I know it! But Kristen, WHO HAS TIME TO SLEEP FOR 8 HOURS?! Many people think they "don't have time" to sleep for eight hours. These people are not prioritizing sleep. Remember when we talked about priorities? Yes, this needs to be a priority. And remember it's about improvement, not perfection. Trim the things out that are not beneficial to your day. Start keeping track of how much time you spend doing everything in your day. The screen time feature on your phone can be quite eye-opening for many people. Social media has damaged our sleep cycles, as has our ability to check our work emails at home.

Let's talk a bit about sleep hygiene. Make sure your bedroom is dark, quiet and relaxing. You shouldn't use screens in your bed. That includes checking social media and work emails. You want your bed to signal rest to your brain. Avoid caffeine in the afternoon. The half-life of caffeine in most people is about 5 hours, so you still have caffeine pushing your eyelids open 10 hours later! Consider some relaxing meditation or yoga before bed to help you wind down.

Some people might win the argument here about not having 8 hours to sleep. If you just had a baby then okay, you win. But your baby won't keep you up forever. You will sleep again, I promise! And teaching your baby to sleep is a wonderful gift you can give them. If you work nights, you win. I have no advice here. I don't work nights and don't know how you do it. Care-takers of the sick, you win. And pat yourself on the back, good job. Students are probably saying, "yeah, we win too!" No, you don't, sorry. Pulling all-nighters is worse for taking tests than getting enough sleep. Sleep is required for taking the material you studied and processing it into your memory. You will do better if you sleep. As for the rest of you, find the excuses you're making for yourself and get rid of them. What is easier than lying in bed to improve your health? You will probably find getting enough sleep helps you complete tasks faster because you are more focused and more capable after a good night's rest. Completing these tasks faster will open up more time in your day for doing things you love.

Pillar 2: Diet

The Diet Restoration phase will require you to eliminate some foods permanently and some foods temporarily. I'm going to throw a lot of information at you here. Don't worry, I'll bring everything together at the end and walk you through the diet process.

Many believe your skin is the largest connection to the outside world, but your gut is in fact the largest connection to the outside world. Your gut is taking in all the external nutrients and toxins and processing them. If you stretched your intestines out, the surface area would cover the size of a tennis court. And unlike your skin that is meant to keep things out, your gut is meant to bring things into your body as well as keep things out. The old saying "you are what you eat" is actually quite literal. It's important that you eat real, whole foods and not processed, packaged garbage.

For many of you, changing your diet will be the most difficult part of this journey. But trust me, it is the most effective. Although it may be a difficult journey, not running to the bathroom with a sudden urge or lying in the fetal position in agony or feeling bloated and constipated for days will be worth it. After some time and consistency on a healthy diet, not only will you have less frequent GI issues, you will start to feel energized, happier, and healthier. I have to give my sugar cravers a bit of a warning though. Changing your diet and significantly reducing your sugar intake will make you feel pretty bad for a few days here and there during the first couple weeks as your body is adjusting to these changes. As you will read below, sugar is an addiction. You will have cravings and some side effects similar to withdrawal. It's very important you fight these cravings. You will overcome that hump very soon and start to feel better. Don't let yourself cheat, not even a little bit. You wouldn't tell a recovering drug addict in rehab to take just one more hit for fun, would you?

I tell many of my patients it is not so much about what you *do* eat, as it is about what you *don't* eat. I got this saying from my favorite aunt. I used to think she was too obsessive over her diet, but she's not the one running to the bathroom on an airplane during take-off due to an SSS. Eating all your vegetables doesn't help much if you follow it with fast food chicken strips, fries and a shake. It's kind of like building a high-rise building with all the right materials, and then filling it with dynamite and lighting a match.

The Diet Restoration process is the toughest and strictest part of this journey. Don't worry, you can do it. The shortest amount of time to do the Diet Restoration is 30 days. If you have significant issues, you may want to extend it to 60 days. You want to choose a time when you can be very in control of your diet. That means not during holidays, weddings, vacations, long work trips, etc. You want to choose 30 days where you can control what ingredients are going into your body. And did I mention you're not drinking alcohol during this time either? So, no happy hours or wine Wednesdays. This process involves two things: permanent elimination of foods I call poisons and temporary elimination of foods I call irritants. The foods we eliminate permanently are foods that harm the body and cause disease. The foods we eliminate temporarily are foods that cause certain people irritation, but are not bad for your health.

Unfortunately, the modern diet is saturated in the foods I call poisons. Eliminating them is a tedious process, but it is the most efficient way to improve your symptoms. I am extremely strict with these foods, but there are times when life requires an exception. I only rarely allow exceptions. Rarely means less than once a month. Some exceptions being: eating at a friend's house (I don't want to be rude, so I eat what they serve unless I am actually allergic) and holidays (you have to live sometimes) and busy work days. After the 4 Week Diet Restoration we can allow these rare exceptions. During Diet Restoration there are **NO EXCEPTIONS**. That's why you must choose a time-frame where you have full control.

A note on busy work days: sometimes you just can't workout, go to work, take care of your kids, walk your dog, do the laundry and cook dinner all in one day. Especially when your dog swallows a tennis ball right before you were about to cook dinner and you have to take him and your two-year-old to the emergency vet! These busy days are happening more and more and opting for fast food can be so tempting. Rather than opting for fast food I do the following. On days I have a little extra time I will double my dinner recipe and freeze one half for the busy weeknight meals. Doubling a recipe usually only adds a few extra minutes. I also have a list of restaurants that we can order out from that have trustworthy ingredients. I may have to order an hour ahead of time rather than drive through in five minutes, but I'd prefer this over poisoning my family. When I do this, I always ask for no salad dressing or condiments and use my own. (As you will read below, dressing and condiments are full of harmful oils).

The Poisons

Let's start with the things I call poisons. These are things that I recommend everyone eliminates from their diet for good. Forever. Never eat them again. The items I list as poisons severely damage your system and are culprits of disease. If you only make one change in this book, this should be it. I won't list the damage caused by each item, as that would take up most of this book. In general, the damage includes: urgency, indigestion, inflammation, fatigue, diarrhea, constipation, skin problems, coronary artery disease, high blood pressure, heart disease, increased risk of diabetes, risk to fetus during pregnancy, infertility, early death, cancer and many more. Yes, you read that right, early death. Remember when I compared your symptoms to an alarm? These symptoms are warning you that your body is not functioning at full capacity. Some of these foods may be confusing to you as the media and government resources such as MyPlate.gov, have promoted use of some of these foods. If you want to take an in depth look at these issues, read *Deep Nutrition* by Catherine Shanahan, MD. She goes into great detail on how the modern diet is depleting our health and how many of the foods recommended as "healthy" are actually killing us.

Toxic Fats and Oils

The simplest way to look at fat is: natural fats are good, processed fats and fried foods are bad. So, French fries are out. Many believe "vegetable oils" are healthy because they have been promoted as a healthy alternative to animal fat. They're made from plants, so they're like totally healthy right? There is immense confusion surrounding these oils. The confusion comes from not understanding chemistry, not understanding the processing these oils go through, and the sugar industry paying off researchers a few decades ago. Let's start with the chemistry first.

Thanks to my food science degree, I have a minor in chemistry. I'm no chemist, but I do remember a few things. It is true that things like canola seeds contain healthy omega-3 and omega-6 fatty acids. These are essential fatty acids, meaning we need them in our diet. Our bodies take these polyunsaturated fatty acids (PUFAs) and mold them into the compounds needed for functions throughout our body. The problem with PUFAs lies with heat. PUFAs, like omega-3 and omega-6, contain double bonds in their carbon chain. These double bonds are highly susceptible to damage via oxidation when heated. These fats have two places where oxygen can enter and react via their double bonds. Once oxygen enters the molecule, it creates a free radical. Free radicals are scary because they are highly reactive and cause a chain reaction like dominoes. Once they enter your body, they jump from PUFA to PUFA creating mutants. This chain reaction not only fries your arteries like fried chicken, but can damage almost every tissue in your body including your gut lining and beneficial bacteria. It's as if we're cooking with an explosive when we cook with these "vegetable oils"… kind of. For comparison, TNT contains 6 locations where oxygen can react giving it it's explosive power. So maybe vegetable oils aren't actually lighting things on fire, but these fats are dangerous when heated, leading to a chain reaction of damaged cells. And you know those damaged cells include your intestinal lining and your microbiome. Not only are they depleting your lining leading to painful digestion, but they are also killing off your beneficial microbes.

You're thinking okay, okay, I won't cook with them, but I still want all those healthy omega-3 and omega-6 fatty acids. I'll use them on my salads! Let's go! Well, I hate to break it to you, these oils are not healthy in any form. The processing is alarming. The refining process involves intense heat, high pressure, and solvents such as hexane. What comes out is a brown, mucky gunk. After this, the gunk goes through about 20 more steps including bleaching and deodorizing to create "vegetable oil." Oils that are "expeller pressed" simply means hexane (or something similar) wasn't used. But, they still undergo all the other processing steps. Most of the healthy oils that once existed are now gone and replaced by a highly reactive oil. Studies on these oils have shown that as much as 5% contain cyclic hydrocarbons and oxyphytosterols. Cyclic hydrocarbons are considered food and environmental contaminants. Many of them are also considered carcinogens. I think most of us know that carcinogens can cause cancer, but what about oxyphytosterols? These are oxidized phytosterols and are mainly produced in the deodorizing stage. The compounds have been found to damage arteries, accumulate in the brain, and thought to increase your risk for Alzheimer's and Multiple Sclerosis (MS).

Once ingested, these oils cause inflammation, free radicals, damaged cells, inflamed arteries, high blood pressure, heart attacks, and erectile dysfunction. Part of my food science degree was learning how the food industry processes food to make it shelf stable. At that time, I may have understood chemistry, but I had very little understanding of how this extreme processing affects physiology and how harmful these processed oils are for the human body. Now I see how consuming these oils are essentially crisping your arteries.

I won't lie to you, these toxic fats are extremely difficult to get rid of if you're buying pre-made or packaged food. Let's be real, these are hard for everyone to get rid of unless you're a homesteader. They are in almost every shelf-stable food you can buy. They even run rampant in "so-called" health foods. This was the final step I took in my gut journey and by far had the biggest effect on my health and energy levels. It was the final key in unlocking my wellness. I wish I knew about these poisons sooner. That's why you are doing this step first. Once I got rid of these fats, I finally felt energized and decreased my GI discomfort drastically. For years, I thought peanut butter didn't agree with me. It turns out peanut butter is just fine when the only ingredients are peanuts and salt. It was the copious amounts of canola and soybean oil found in almost every brand of popular peanut butter that didn't agree with my system.

Once I started searching for these toxic fats on food labels, I found that I was drowning in these oils. I found them in almost everything I bought that was not either produce, nuts, meat, or eggs. Common culprits are highly processed foods, cereals, pre-made snacks, bars, crackers, hummus, coffee creamer, non-dairy milk, salad dressing, protein powder, condiments, granola, pastries, muffins, junk food, fast food and on and on the list goes. You should be reading every food label and searching for all the toxic fats in the ingredient section (listed below).

For most items I have been able to find a product that does not contain toxic oils. Some I have not, or the one I have found is quadruple the price. In that case, I will make my own or decide I don't need it. One of these items is hummus. I cannot find a moderately priced hummus that does not contain soybean or canola oil. So, I make my own with a can of chickpeas, olive oil, and lemon in a food processor and it takes less than five minutes. I eyeball the olive oil and lemon and sometimes add something for flavor like a jalapeño or garlic. I have decided to go without store bought salad dressing. I use olive oil, balsamic, lemon, apple cider vinegar, or some sort of combination of these.

For those of you that think you are the picture of health and can't figure out why you feel terrible, this is probably it. These oils are so much cheaper than olive oil that they are found in most foods you might consider health foods. My two biggest surprises were plant-based milk and hummus. I thought, "I'm so darn healthy adding plant-based milk to my smoothie, congratulations to me." Then I discovered most, not all, are full of poison. Read the labels. And hummus! Hummus is supposed to be chickpeas and olive oil. That's it. I never even thought about reading the label. Now, hummus is chickpeas and soybean oil, sunflower oil, or canola oil. These processed toxins are so cheap they are replacing almost every healthy oil on the market. You are not safe just because you shop at health food stores. This is happening in products in every type of store.

Good News!!! Not all fats are bad. In fact, many fats are good and part of a healthy diet!

Bad News!!! Toxic fats are abundant in modern food.

Good	Toxic
ANIMAL FATS BUTTER OLIVE OIL PEANUT OIL PALM OIL UNREFINED, COLD PRESSED OILS	PROCESSED FAT INCLUDING TRANS FAT AND NON-BUTTER SPREADS CANOLA OIL SOYBEAN OIL SUNFLOWER OIL COTTONSEED OIL CORN OIL GRAPESEED OIL SAFFLOWER OIL "VEGETABLE OIL"

Read every food label, even labels of foods that are a "health food." Eliminate all foods that contain toxic fats.

Note: many more oils can be healthy if they are cold pressed and unrefined. But these are very hard to come by. A study found 82% of avocado oil imported to the US was either rancid (poison), mixed with other toxic oils, or not avocado oil at all. Palm oil is controversial. If you can find reputable source, then most research says it's safe to use.

Added Sugar

Sugar. Everyone loves sugar. Literally, everyone. Our bodies are designed to love sugar because it fuels our cells. Sugar in modest amounts is not a problem. Sugar in the modern diet is a major problem. Sugar is added to just about every single food we eat, from the obvious sweets to sandwich bread, pasta sauce, salad dressing, non-dairy milk, condiments, salsa, yogurt, fast food, etc. I can't name everything, because frankly it is in almost everything.

Sugar is tricky. We need it, many natural and healthy foods have it, but modern society is swimming in it and it is quite literally killing us. If you go back to hunter gatherer days, sugar was a rare treat. Found only in fruit that came around a couple times a year, honey that was only ingested when they were lucky enough to find a beehive, and milk. I'm probably missing a couple things, but you get the point. Today, sugar is everywhere. Most Americans have no idea how much sugar they are eating.

To keep things short, I will summarize the damage of sugar. This is another topic discussed in depth in *Deep Nutrition*. If you want a full brief on the dangers of sugar, read that book. Too much sugar leads to: diabetes, obesity, hormone dysregulation, accelerated aging process, decreased mood, weakened bones, memory loss, dementia, hardened arteries (high blood pressure, heart attacks, heart disease etc), birth defects, infertility, headaches, higher rates of chemical dependencies, dulled senses, increased cravings, etc. That's a long list of problems and I didn't even name them all. You know if it's causing all that is listed above it is also causing digestive issues. Sugar feeds that "bad" bacteria in your gut and prevents your system from breaking food down appropriately leading to endless problems when it comes to digestion.

I'm assuming most of you have heard the statement by now that sugar is more addicting than cocaine. It is the most consumed addicting substance worldwide. Something you may not have heard yet is that high sugar intake increases the risk of chemical dependency. Watching Americans shove their kids full of juice, sugar filled bars (most snack bars for kids are glorified candy bars), sugar filled crackers, sweets, candy, ice cream, daily dessert, and sugar filled cereal is heartbreaking to me. These kids are being set up for a lifelong addiction to a substance that will cause disease and early death. They are also being primed to be more susceptible to drug addiction later in life. You probably think I'm being dramatic because feeding kids sugar is the norm now. Just because it is the norm doesn't mean it's good. Smoking cigarettes while pregnant used to be the norm too, but we don't do that anymore now do we?

Sugar is an actual addiction, so there's no doubt it will be tough to kick. But, it will change your life. Remember this will be the hard part where you won't feel good during those first two weeks and your body is telling you to cheat. Don't let your cravings take over. The few days of discomfort will be over soon and you will be on the road to healing with less public bathroom stops.

You should be reading food labels and looking for the "added sugar" section. If there is added sugar don't eat it. Added sugar is everywhere, but you can usually find an option that does not have added sugar. There are some foods that even I will admit are tough to eat without added sugar. One of those being plain yogurt. Instead of adding sugar I will add fresh or frozen berries or fruit. The fiber in the berries or fruit allows the sugar to absorb slower and you have the benefit of vitamins and antioxidants. I tend to avoid things that are high in sugar even if naturally occurring, especially juice. I never give my kids juice. It is a straight shot of sugar.

I do eat some natural sugar. Things that have natural sugar (not added sugar) that I commonly eat include: plain full fat Greek yogurt, cream in my coffee (plain cream, not creamer), manuka honey (a teaspoon when sick), produce (fresh fruit, berries, citrus, vegetables), full fat milk (added to smoothies or home-made recipes), honey and maple syrup (added to marinades and dressings in very small amounts).

I also have to comment on the new fad of "sugar-free" baked goods and bars that are a favorite on Pinterest. There is a swarm of recipes claiming to be sugar-free, yet add a gallon of maple syrup or honey. Yes, technically they are free of cane sugar, but maple syrup and honey are forms of sugar.

While on the subject of sugar, simple carbs are a complicated topic. They fall into their own category. Because they are digested into sugars and raise your blood sugar, I'll mention them here. These are things like bread, pasta, cereal, quick oatmeal, most crackers, white rice, and many more. I don't put them on my poison list. But I do put them on my limit list. Think of them as sugar. They are quickly digested into simple sugars and released throughout your system as sugar. These are best eaten in small quantities and on a limited basis. Personally, I eat these items less than once a week and some not at all.

Artificial Additives

There are so many food additives that fall into the poison category there are too many to mention. I will mention categories to look out for and list the main ones below in the food charts. These shorten your lifespan, increase disease, destroy your gut, and increase your symptoms similar to toxic oils.

Fat Free

Don't choose items labeled fat free. These are filled with artificial chemicals, thickeners, and sweeteners that fall under the poison category. We only consume full fat milk, yogurt, sour cream, cheese, etc. in our home.

Sugar Free

Candy is candy, soda is soda, junk food is junk food. Sugar free substitutes are just as bad if not worse for your system than the full sugar item. Your body does not know what to do with artificial sweeteners and they cause dysregulation and fall into the poison category.

Artificial Flavoring

Eat things with real flavor, not artificial. Again these are poisons.

Buzz Words

Processed junk food labeled with a healthy buzz word like "keto," "paleo," and whatever other fad diet is popular at the time is usually filled with food additives. Don't let these trick you. Read the label.

If a natural form of a food contains fat, and a company is selling a "fat free" version of that food, then you should think of the term "fat free" as "chemical filled". To make the food still taste and look palatable, they add fillers. These fillers are thickeners like gums, chemicals, flours and sugar. These chemicals destroy your intestinal lining and microbiome. Rather than leading to a feeling of fullness and satiety, they lead to increased sugar intake, more cravings, and dysbiosis by feeding your bad microbes. Buy the full fat version, not the fat free or low-fat version. Eat fat you say? Yes. Natural, unprocessed fats contain essential fatty acids required for proper brain function, nervous system function, GI function, immune responses, hormone production, and building cell membranes. Animal fat contains the fat-soluble vitamins A, D, E, and K. Fat and cholesterol leads to a feeling of fullness and suppresses hunger. These fatty acids are essential for a strong and healthy gut lining to aid digestion. Again, I'm talking about natural fats here, not processed trans fats. Processed trans fats should never be part of your diet. Always read your food labels.

This is a good place to talk about fad diets like keto, paleo, carnivore, etc. Many of my clients find this is where their problem lies. Many of these diets are great. They can lower disease risk, help people lose weight, improve health, and even improve gut health. The problem doesn't lie within the diet itself (depending on the diet obviously). Things like keto or paleo were started with the intention of consuming whole, nutritious foods. The problem lies with processed food and marketing. Let's take keto for example. The keto diet in short is high fat and low carb. It forces your body to use fat for fuel rather than glucose. This is great when you are eating whole foods. The problem comes when companies take hold of these diets and process foods that contain chemicals that allow them to still be called "keto" or "paleo" or whatever the diet is. Then these companies market chemical filled foods as "keto" or "paleo" and trick you into eating poison. Processed food can contain xanthan gum, sorbitol, "sugar alcohol", erythritol, artificial sweeteners, natural sweeteners, and many more and still claim the title of keto, paleo, etc. Not all of these fillers are chemicals or even bad for your health, but all of these can upset your gut microbiome and lead to more digestive symptoms. One of the reasons the carnivore diet can be so successful is because it forces people to eliminate all the food additives and poisons by just eating meat. If you don't know what the carnivore diet is, you just eat meat. That's it. Like I said, it's not always about what you do eat, but also about what you don't eat. Always read the label and aim for whole foods not processed foods. Just because the package claims it's healthy doesn't mean it is.

Sugar free is another big problem. Many of the "sugar-free" labeled foods are artificial chemicals. These destroy your microbiome, and some have been found to increase risk of cancer. Many foods are also now adding stevia and monk fruit. Now, there aren't studies that I know of that state stevia or monk fruit are necessarily bad for your health. But, my issue with these products is: sweet is sweet. If you keep feeding your sweet cravings with sugar substitutes, you will keep craving sweet things. We want to end your sweet craving cycle and allow your body to want healthy, whole, unprocessed foods instead of diet soda, "sugar-free" coffee drinks, and poison-filled energy drinks. In addition, most monk fruit sweeteners are mixed with erythritol to make it look more like sugar. Erythritol can increase your digestive issues and cause things like diarrhea, bloating, cramps, and gas. Remember, always read your labels. Always!

Lastly, artificial flavoring is artificial. There's not much to add here. It's a chemical like those discussed above. You should eat real food with real flavor.

Fast Food

Why is fast food bad? Because it is filled with poison. Which poisons? Toxic fat, sugar, and artificial food additives.

That's really all I have to say about fast food. You just read all the reasons why toxic fats are poison, why sugar is poison, and why artificial additives are poison. There is not much left to say. There are so many fast food companies I'm not going to list them. You know what they are in your area. Avoid them. Don't pay for poison. Do your research on restaurants. A very popular sandwich company claiming to be "healthy" has so much sugar in their sandwich bread that Ireland labels their bread as a pastry.

Summary of Poisons

I don't doubt this stage will be difficult for some of you. It was difficult for me. You have to completely retrain your brain how to think about food. Though it is difficult, I did it and many of my patients have done it as well. You can do it too. Some foods are extremely addicting and your brain tricks you into thinking that processed food tastes better. Once you retrain your brain to view these as poison (because that's what they are), your body will no longer crave them and even reject them. I find with my private clients that the biggest challenge doesn't come with adding nutritious foods to their diet. They usually don't struggle too much adding fruits and vegetables for example. The challenge comes with *not* eating their go-to poison filled foods. This is because the gut bacteria in your GI tract send signals to your brain to crave the foods they crave. When we say you are "feeding a craving" you are quite literally feeding the bacteria that is causing the craving. If you keep feeding the sugar-craving bacteria, then the sugar-craving colony in your gut will grow and grow pushing out healthy microbes. If you eat diverse, nutritious, whole foods then you will be feeding the beneficial microbes allowing more diversity. Remember your GI tract is like a garden. When you grow a garden, you water it and fertilize it. You don't dump Roundup on it.

After eliminating these poisons from my body for just a short time, the thought of foods I used to frequently eat and love started sickening me. I used to absolutely love a specific coffee creamer with a passion. I wouldn't drink coffee without it. I haven't had it in over 10 years at this point. I was out of town and this specific creamer was the only "cream" available. It tasted so awful to me that I dumped my coffee out after one sip and chose black coffee instead. Removing poisons from our body is a forever change and I know you can do it! We will discuss the elimination process of these poisons at the end of the chapter.

The Irritants

Irritants are foods that irritate your system. This is very personal. They are not foods that are bad for your health, rather foods that don't sit right with you. Irritants can cause gas, bloating, indigestion, diarrhea, constipation, or heartburn. They can also cause skin problems such as itching, eczema and acne. The good thing about irritants is that they don't have to be eliminated forever. Most people find that once they heal their system they are able to eat most of their irritants on a moderate basis. If you follow my Instagram or blog you will see I don't promote low FODMAP (explained later) or similar types of elimination diets. I don't promote these as long-term solutions however, I do use these as a short-term tool. Eliminating irritating foods for a short time does a few things. One, it gives many people immediate relief. Two, it gives your body a break from constant exposure to the irritant allowing your body to heal. Now, we don't eliminate these foods forever because: many of these foods are very healthy and we don't want to keep you from eating healthy foods. Once you allow your body to heal and promote healthy gut bacteria most people are able to digest these foods without issue. Some of these foods may also be a true allergy. If you have never had an allergy test, it's worth considering.

Factors Contributing to Irritation

The main reason most healthy foods cause irritation is because you don't have the proper gut bacteria to help you break them down. Another reason is because your gut lining is so damaged it can't handle large amounts. The compounds that can be irritating to the gut lining typically possess certain characteristics or properties that trigger a response from the body's immune system or sensory receptors. Here are some factors that can contribute to the irritancy of compounds:

i. **Chemical Structure:** Compounds with certain chemical structures may have irritant properties. For example, substances with reactive functional groups or high acidity/alkalinity can damage tissues upon contact, leading to irritation.

ii. **pH:** Extreme pH levels, either highly acidic or highly alkaline, can disrupt the pH balance of the skin, mucous membranes, or other tissues, causing irritation and inflammation.

iii. **Allergenicity:** Some compounds can act as allergens, triggering allergic reactions in susceptible individuals.

iv. **Concentration:** The concentration or dose of a compound can influence its irritant potential. Even substances that are generally safe at low concentrations can become irritating or toxic at higher concentrations.

v. **Duration of Exposure:** Prolonged or repeated exposure to a compound can increase the likelihood of irritation. Continuous contact with irritants can lead to cumulative damage and chronic inflammation.

vi. **Individual Sensitivity:** The sensitivity of an individual can vary, with some people being more prone to irritation than others. Factors such as age, pre-existing conditions, and genetic predispositions can influence individual sensitivity to irritants.

Eliminating Irritants

Everyone will eliminate the irritants listed below for 14 days. Don't worry, there's a comprehensive food chart at the end of the chapter. These items are very abundant in modern food. They are also items that people categorize as "not weird" or tell me, "it's definitely not that" because they don't want to give it up or it's so ingrained in their routine that giving it up seems too difficult to them. Or it's so common they can't fathom it could be making them feel bad. Let's be clear here: constant symptoms are from constant ingestion of irritating substances. Why am I hitting this point so hard? Because this is where I find the most pushback from clients. Such a common thing I hear is "I didn't eat anything weird." Yes, I know. Having constant digestive symptoms isn't from "weird" foods. It's from your common "go-to" foods. We need to figure out what they are and what triggers you personally. And remember this is only a temporary change while you heal.

1. **Wheat, Barley, Rye, Gluten:** The modern diet is so filled with wheat and gluten that most people eat it for every meal, snack, and dessert. A moderate intake may not cause problems for many. But an excess on a damaged system can wreak havoc. Barley and rye also contain gluten so it is best to just eliminate all three during the Restoration phase as many have digestive issues with gluten and don't realize it. A moderate amount of gluten may not cause problems, but eating

gluten all day long can overwhelm your system. This was the first thing I eliminated in my elimination diet phase. I realized I ate wheat all day long. Breakfast, lunch, dinner, snacks, dessert. When I cut it out, not only did my digestion issues improve, but my skin got clearer, my fatigue improved and I no longer felt brain fog.

2. **Coffee:** Coffee is an extremely irritating substance. Coffee is often listed as one of the top 10 foods associated with IBS. A 2021 study in *Frontiers of Nutrition* found that those who drink coffee weekly had a 44% greater risk of IBS than those who don't drink coffee. The compounds in coffee irritate the stomach lining causing everything from heartburn, to diarrhea, urgency, and indigestion. These compounds increase gastric acid secretion leading to stomach pain. They also stimulate muscle activity in the colon leading to urgency. Eliminating coffee has made night and day differences in many people. And most people are able to add it back in once their system has healed. Caffeine alone is a slight irritant as well. I know most of you don't want to go through your day caffeine free. If you want to go above and beyond then eliminate all caffeine for 30 days. It will be a great cleanse

for your gut and your brain and you will probably realize you don't need caffeine every day. But if you're not an overachiever, opt for green tea to get your caffeine fix for these 14 days. Coffee is one of those foods that my patients like to fight me on. "I've had coffee every day for 30 years, it's definitely not that." If you're filling your system with an irritant every day for 30 years, it probably is "that." So, toughen up and suffer with your first world problem for 14 days.

3. **Chocolate and Cacao**: Most chocolate falls into the high sugar no-no category. But dark chocolate 60% and higher has many antioxidants, so I do eat it. But, this is an irritant for many so we will give your system a break. This includes pure cacao and cacao nibs for those of you who add that to your smoothies, oatmeal or snacks. Chocolate can contain lactose, caffeine, and sugar. All things that can cause a flareup and spark digestive pain.

4. **Garlic and Onions:** I put these in the same category because they are often found together in foods, sauces and condiments. Both these ingredients are extremely

irritating to the damaged gut and are so abundant. They are in so many hot sauces, dressings, marinades, sauces, pasta sauces, it's hard to go without them. Without the proper gut flora to break these down, they cause painful bloating in many people. On the other hand, these also feed beneficial bacteria, which is why we don't want to eliminate them forever. Once your beneficial bacteria colony is flourishing and able to break down these foods properly, then you can add these back in without issue.

5. **Spicy Food:** Spicy food has many health benefits from a substance called capsaicin that includes weight loss, endorphin release, fighting inflammation, and acting as an antioxidant. I think everyone probably knows spicy food is not great for people with digestion issues. Capsaicin is thought to "burn" your intestines in a similar way to how it "burns" your mouth leading to aggravation of certain nerve fibers and heartburn. Give your system a little break from the pain. Once your GI system heals, we can add spicy food back in and gain all those wonderful benefits from capsaicin.

6. **Liquid Dairy**: This is a common cause of digestive issues. Even just a little cream in your coffee (good thing I took that away too) can cause problems. Both diarrhea and constipation, as well as skin issues can be caused by milk and cream. Some people find they can tolerate some dairy and not others. Liquid dairy contains the most lactose compared to other dairy such as yogurt and cheese where much of the lactose has been converted to lactic acid. That's why some people can handle cheese, but not drink a glass of milk. You can consider eliminating all dairy for a short while depending on how much dairy you consume.

7. **Alcohol:** This is the thing that stops some people from trying to get better. Getting rid of alcohol is hard, but so necessary in this journey. Alcohol is an irritant for everyone, even people that don't complain of digestive issues. All alcohol in larger quantities can cause erosion, paralysis, and hemorrhaging of the smooth muscle of the stomach. Beer causes bloating and contains gluten. Wine has many compounds in it that act as irritants and can cause heartburn and indigestion. The new seltzer craze usually has artificial poisons in them. Hard alcohol is just

a straight irritant to your gut lining. I don't tell you to give it up permanently because that's something that many people are not willing to do. I do require you to give it up completely for 14 days. After 14 days you can add it back in small quantities. If you can't give up alcohol for 14 days to heal your gut lining, it may be time to consider talking to a professional about that. I try to encourage everyone to keep alcohol out of their diet as long as they can as it is such a strong irritant.

8. **Sweeteners:** We know why we can't have artificial sweeteners: poison. But we're also going to eliminate natural sweeteners. We want to end the cycle of your body constantly craving sugar. Eating things with added sweeteners, even if natural, keeps this cycle going. We want to eliminate your bacteria colonies craving these sweet foods so that your healthy colonies can grow. Sweeteners are also the culprit of many digestive issues. They can cause heartburn, diarrhea, bloating, constipation, and gas depending on the person. They are listed in the chart below.

9. **FODMAPs** are a group of fibers and carbohydrates that cause severe digestive pain and issues for some people. This stands for fermentable oligosaccharides, disaccharides, monosaccharides, and polyols (these are listed in the food charts at the end of the chapter). Just eliminating FODMAPs for as little as seven days can make a night and day difference in some people. Many of these foods are very good for you, so we will slowly add them back in and hopefully you can identify your personal triggers. Once your gut has had some time to rest and heal and your gut microbiome is healthy again, it's likely that these will no longer cause problems for you. Why? Because if you cultivate healthy bacteria in your gut, then your bacteria will break down these foods for you and help you absorb all their beneficial nutrients. At the very least, you should be able to eat them in modest amounts. It can be a big challenge to cook without high FODMAP foods. There are many low FODMAP cookbooks out there with healthy recipes. Many of you may have tried this already as it is promoted in almost every IBS resource there is. You might be thinking, ugh Kristen, I already tried this and you said you don't promote it! Yes, yes I know what I said. However, eliminating these for a short time can improve symptoms right off the bat. I don't promote this

as a *healing* mechanism for IBS or a long-term solution. This is only a temporary change to get symptoms in check, identify triggers, give your body a rest, and eventually you can eat these foods again.

Optional Irritants:

Below are some additional foods that may cause irritation. Eliminate these optional irritants below based on your symptoms as well as what you eat often. If you eat it often you should give your system a break. If you're having digestive issues often, it's due to something you're eating often (yes, I'm making that point again). Find your symptoms below and look at the foods listed. In addition to the irritants listed above, eliminate the foods below for 14 days that correspond to your symptoms.

- **Heartburn:** Tomatoes, tomato sauce, black pepper, bacon, sausage, peppermint (breath mints often have poisons in them and bloat causing sweeteners), citrus, black tea, all peppers

- **Bloating/indigestion/gas:** Carbonated drinks, medium FODMAP foods, high fiber (fiber is necessary in the diet, but it should be added in slowly to prevent gas and discomfort), oatmeal

- **Diarrhea:** All dairy, tomato sauce, oatmeal, all caffeine, all peppers even if not overly spicy including bell peppers

- **Constipation:** Dairy, add fiber to your diet slowly via adding high fiber foods or by adding psyllium husk daily

- **Diarrhea/Constipation Combo:** All dairy, citrus, tomato sauce, tomatoes, oatmeal, all peppers, eggs

Summary

Again, irritants are not bad for health in general. They just may not sit right with you personally. The irritants are a temporary change. We just need to identify your triggers and allow your body time to heal and take a break from your triggers. Once your digestive lining is healed and your microbiome is balanced again you will likely be able to process these foods without issue. Many people are able to add their triggers back in moderation after taking a break. Most people are also surprised at the new foods they discover during this phase that they love!

Hydration

The last thing I will mention about diet is hydration. Hydration is another forever change. You should be drinking plenty of water throughout the day. Our bodies are made up of 60% water. Staying adequately hydrated is vital for proper functions in the body including nutrient transport, temperature regulation, removing waste, metabolism, lubricating our joints, blood pressure, electrolyte balance, and appropriate GI function. Regarding gut health, it helps your gut properly break down foods, prevents constipation, and helps keep your bowel movements regular. There is no one size fits all for how much water you should drink. Everyone is different. Hydration level also depends on the amount of exercise you get, what kind of foods you eat, and what kind of climate you live in. Most people do not consume nearly enough water. If you experience any of the following then you likely are not getting enough water: darker urine, urine with a strong odor, dry mouth, headaches, poor concentration, fatigue, or using the toilet less than four times per day. Waiting until you're thirsty to drink means you're already dehydrated.

Because hydration depends on climate, body composition, and the foods you eat I recommend talking to your physician about what amount is right for you. You can also use a hydration calculator online. What I do recommend is everyone starting their day with 16 oz of water (before anything else including coffee or tea) and keep a water bottle close by throughout the day. Sip water throughout the day rather than gulping large amounts at once. Try to take more water in during the morning and early afternoon to avoid get up at night to use the bathroom multiple times. On days you exercise be sure to increase your water intake. If you don't enjoy drinking plain water then add a squeeze of lemon, lime, or orange. You could also try infusing your water overnight with mint, cucumber, or berries. Don't add store-bought water "enhancers" or flavorings. These usually contain dyes, chemicals and sweeteners that fall into the poison category or cause painful bloating or cramping. They also feed your sweet craving.

THE STEPS TO RESTORE

Something I hear more often than I'd like to with my patients when they have a digestive incident is: "I didn't eat anything weird." This comment absolutely drives me crazy. Oh wait, did I say that already? Yes, I know, I did! Why am I saying it again? Because I bet while you were reading the list above you said to yourself "No way Kristen, that's not causing my pain." Why do I know this? Because everyone brings this up to me! Or "sorry Kristen, that's a non-negotiable for me. I need my latte every day." That's fine. You can have non-negotiables, but realize you might not get the results you're hoping for. And let's be real, 14 days isn't that long. You might even discover new foods you like even better! Have an open mind. You can do almost anything for 14 days.

If you are having digestive issues on a regular basis, it is not something weird or unusual you are eating that is causing this. It is something you are eating on a regular basis. Please keep this in mind as we go through this process. Remember to look at everything you consume including beverages, gum, mints, vitamins, supplements. Below you will find the process of eliminating all poisons, and temporarily

95

eliminating the irritants and slowly adding them back in. The food charts on the following pages will help you stay on track.

This is where having an open mind is important. It's usually much harder for clients to give up something they're used to than to add something they're not used to. For example, it's easy to start adding a vegetable for dinner, but much harder to give up fries. Just remember your poisons are killing your cells and microbes. The poisons are also increasing your risk for disease and premature death. Reframe your mindset around food and strive to eat things that nourish you rather than poison you.

A note for my high sugar eaters and heavy alcohol drinkers: These first 14 days may be difficult and involve headaches and cravings. You may need to add an extra week before adding foods back in. Remember when you feed the craving you are feeding the bad bacteria in your gut.

Some of you might be looking at this and saying "wow Kristen, this is kind of like….. A LOT to do at once." Feeling overwhelmed with a transformative process is normal. I encourage you to give a try. The faster you dive in, the faster you will feel better. Meal planning is key here. If you feel like you need more of a baby step process then start by just eliminating the poisons. This will likely help some of your symptoms and you will be on your way to less risk for all kinds of health issues by getting these things out of your diet. After two to three weeks of no poisons, then take the next step and eliminate the irritants for 14 days.

Step 1: Give yourself the opportunity to sleep 7 to 8 hours every night.

Step 2: Go through your kitchen, read all your food labels and eliminate everything that contains a poison. If you have a hard time letting go, think about your premature death and pain. That might help.

Step 3: Sequester all the irritants and optional irritants. Don't throw these away as we will be slowly adding them back in later.

Step 4: Stay hydrated. Start each day with a glass of water and drink water throughout the day.

Step 5: After 14 days of elimination, you can add one irritant back in every three days and record your symptoms. If you find a trigger, eliminate that food for 90 days to allow healing. Then try again.

30 DAYS TO RESTORE

DAY 1	Start the full elimination diet of poisons, irritants, and optional irritants (food chart on following pages). Remember to use your FSJ daily.
DAY 2 TO DAY 14	Hold strong on your elimination diet. It will be hard, but I know you can do it. Remember to drink lots of water.
DAY 15	Add one irritant back in and record the results over the next two days in your FSJ. If you have digestive issues flare up, eliminate that food for 90 days then try again.
DAY 18	Add another irritant and record results. Note: I don't recommend adding coffee and alcohol back in the same week as they are both strong irritants.
DAY 21	Add another irritant and record results.
DAY 24	Add another irritant and record results.
DAY 27	Add another irritant and record results.
DAY 30	Add another irritant and record results. You made it! Congratulations! How do you feel? Did you feel like garbage sometimes and blame me for your pain? Thats okay. Now you can thank me when you don't run to the bathroom three times on your next date.

FOOD GUIDE: Poisons

Poisons Eliminate Permanently		Healthy Replacements	
Oils/Fats		Oils/Fats	
• Processed fat including trans fat and non-butter spreads • Canola oil • Soybean oil	• Corn oil • Grapeseed oil • Safflower oil • "Vegetable oil" • Cottonseed oil • Sunflower oil	• Animal fats • Olive oil • Peanut oil	• Butter • Palm oil • Coconut oil
Added Sugar Sweeteners		Foods that are naturally sweet such as fresh or frozen fruit	
Artificial/Chemicals		Natural	
• Fat free • Artificial sweeteners • Artificial flavor • Buzzword junk food • Aspartame • Sucralose • Acesulfame K • Saccharin • Aluminum • Nitrites	• Nitrites • Nitrates • Potassium bromate • Propyl Paraben • BHA • Propyl gallate • Theobromine • Artificial coloring • Diacetyl • Phosphates • Many more	• Full fat products (rather than fat free or low fat) • Nitrate free meats • Natural flavoring	
Junk Food		Whole, Non-Processed Foods	
• Fast food • Candy • Ice cream • Frozen yogurt • Fried food • Processed food • Sugary cereal • Most snack bars • Juice • Syrup	• Pastries • Cookies • Cake • Cupcakes • Pancakes • Whipped topping • Flavored oatmeal • Waffles • Muffins • Jelly/jam	• Cook at home • Do your research on your favorite restaurants • Meat • Eggs • Oatmeal • Vegetables • Fruit • Full fat dairy	• Homemade whipped cream with no sugar added • Homemade smoothies • Nuts/seeds • Peanut Butter • Quinoa • Wild rice

Food Guide: Irritants

Irritants Eliminate for 14 Days		Healthy Replacements	
Wheat, Barley, Rye, Gluten		**Starches/Grains**	
• Pasta • Crackers • Bars	• Bread • Cereal • Desserts • Many more	• Potatoes • Sweet potatoes • Oatmeal • Quinoa	• Wild Rice • Lentils • Beans
Coffee		**Green Tea**	
Chocolate/Cacao/Cacao Nibs		**Other antioxidants or crunchy toppings such as berries and nuts**	
• Garlic • Onions • Spicy		• Turmeric • Cumin • Cinnamon • Cardamom • Allspice	• Mustard powder • Lemon pepper • Paprika • Smoked paprika
Liquid Dairy		**Plant based milk with no added oils or poisons**	
Alcohol			
• Beer • Wine • Hard liquor	• Mixed Drinks • Seltzers	• Water • Sparkling water	• Tea • Shrubs (vinegar based drink)
Sweeteners		**Naturally Sweet Foods**	
• Sorbitol • Xylitol • Stevia	• Monk fruit • Many others	• Fruit	
High FODMAPs (listed below)		**Low FODMAPs Medium FODMAPs in small quantities**	
Optional Irritants			
• All caffeine • Tomatoes/tomato sauce • Citrus • Black pepper • Bacon/sausage	• Peppermint • All peppers • Oatmeal • All Dairy • Eggs • Medium FODMAP	• Herbal tea • Quinoa • Wild rice • Sweet potatoes • Try new spices • Non-carbonated drinks	• Oats soaked overnight • Low FODMAPs

Food Guide: FODMAPs

High FODMAPs	Low FODMAPs

Fruit

High FODMAPs	Low FODMAPs
• Apples • Mangoes	• Banana • Lemons
• Apricots • Nectarines	• Blueberries • Limes
• Blackberries • Peaches	• Cantaloupe • Mandarin
• Boysenberries • Pears	• Clementine • Orange
• Cherries • Persimmons	• Coconut • Papaya
• Currants • Plums	• Dragon fruit • Passion fruit
• Dates • Prunes	• Grapes • Pineapple
• Figs • Tamarillo	• Guava • Raspberries
• Grapefruit • Watermelon	• Honeydew • Rhubarb
	• Kiwifruit • Strawberries

High FODMAPs — Fruit: Apples, Apricots, Blackberries, Boysenberries, Cherries, Currants, Dates, Figs, Grapefruit, Mangoes, Nectarines, Peaches, Pears, Persimmons, Plums, Prunes, Tamarillo, Watermelon

High FODMAPs — Vegetables and Legumes: Artichokes, Asparagus, Cauliflower, Garlic, Leeks, Mushrooms, Onion, Garlic, Shallots, Beans, Peas, Snap peas, Snow peas, Soybeans

High FODMAPs — Grains: Rye, Barley, Wheat

High FODMAPs — Protein: Silken Tofu

High FODMAPs — Other: Pistachios, Cashews, Cottage cheese, Milk Yogurt, Agave, Honey, Chicory root, Chamomile tea, Fennel tea, Oolong tea, Inulin

Low FODMAPs — Fruit: Banana, Blueberries, Cantaloupe, Clementine, Coconut, Dragon fruit, Grapes, Guava, Honeydew, Kiwifruit, Lemons, Limes, Mandarin, Orange, Papaya, Passion fruit, Pineapple, Raspberries, Rhubarb, Strawberries

Low FODMAPs — Vegetables and Legumes: Arugula, Bamboo, Bok Choy, Bell Peppers, Carrots, Chives, Collard greens, Cabbages, Chilis, Cucumber, Eggplant, Endive, Fennel, Ginger, Green beans, Kale, Leeks, Lettuce, Okra, Nori seaweed, Spaghetti Squash, Spinach, Olives, Parsnips, Potatoes, Radishes, Scallions, Squash, Swiss chard, Tomatoes, Turnips, Watercress, Water Chestnuts, Zucchini

Low FODMAPs — Grains: Rice, Buckwheat, Cornmeal, Corn flour, Millet, Oats, Polenta, Quinoa, Tapioca

Low FODMAPs — Protein: Animal based: grass fed beef, pork, fish, free range chicken, etc., Firm tofu, Tempeh

Sample Meal Plan

Note: we are all different sizes and have different goals which is why I don't provide portions in the example meal plan.

Remember to read your labels! Don't blindly buy gluten free pasta and think it's healthy. Look at the ingredients first. That goes for every food or drink you consume.

Meal	Day 1	Day 2	Day 3
Breakfast	Eggs over arugula with blueberries	Eggs with half an avocado (medium FODMAP food)	Oatmeal with: collagen powder, hemp seeds, chia seeds, peanut butter
Snack	Walnuts	Banana and peanut butter	Half an avocado
Lunch	Protein Smoothie: berries, kale, spinach, protein powder (without poisons), peanut butter, hemp seeds, chia seeds, almond milk	Leftover pasta	Leftover salmon and veggies
Snack	Cucumbers, Carrots and Hummus	Pecans	Strawberries and blueberries
Dinner	Gluten Free Pasta with: olive oil, jarred roasted red peppers, zucchini and parsley	Salmon, baked sweet potato (small portion as this is a medium FODMAP food), and roasted fennel, tomatoes, zucchini, kalamata olives, and capers tossed in olive oil	Chicken lettuce wraps

Day 1 Pasta:

Gluten free pasta

Olive oil to preference

Shredded parmesan to preference

Jarred roasted red peppers – sliced

1 to 2 zucchinis sliced

Parsley chopped

Cook pasta according to directions. Add sliced zucchini to pasta for the last 2 minutes of cooking. Place red peppers in colander. Drain pasta over red peppers to heat them up. Mix in olive oil and parsley. Top with parmesan.

Day 2 Salmon

Salmon filet

1 Sweet potato

1 fresh fennel bulb, white part sliced

1 lb cherry tomatoes

1 zucchini sliced

½ cup kalamata olives

2 tablespoons of capers or to taste

1 tablespoon of fresh dill

2 tablespoons of olive oil

Grill salmon and top with chopped fresh dill. Bake sweet potato and top with butter or coconut oil. Place all veggies, olives and capers in bowl and mix with olive oil. Spread on sheet pan and season with salt and pepper. Cover with foil and bake for 15 minutes at 450. Remove foil and stir and bake uncovered for another 15 minutes.

Day 3 Chicken Lettuce Wraps

1 tablespoon olive oil

1 tablespoon grated ginger

1 lb ground chicken

1 carrot shredded

1 bell pepper chopped

$\frac{1}{2}$ cup water chestnuts chopped

$\frac{1}{4}$ cup scallion

2 tablespoons oyster sauce

1 tablespoon gluten free soy sauce

2 heads butter lettuce

Chopped cilantro to taste

Heat oil in skillet over medium heat. Adder ginger and stir for 1 minute. Add chicken and cook for 2 minutes. Add carrots, bell pepper, water chestnuts, scallions and cook for 1 minute. Add oyster sauce, soy sauce, and sesame oil and cook until chicken is cooked through. Place stir fry in lettuce cups and garnish with cilantro.

Summary

How are you feeling? Mad at me? Was that a hard 30 days? Did you blame me for your painful days and cravings? Now you can thank me as things get better and your gut starts to heal (you're welcome). Remember to continue your seven to eight hours of sleep, hydration, and keep those poisons out of your diet. As far as the irritants go, keep your personal triggers out for at least 90 days and then you can try them again. All other irritants that are not triggers for you can be eaten again.

Chapter 6: Rebuild

Pillar 3: Supplements

This section is about rebuilding your intestinal lining and microbiome for healthy digestion. Before diving into these supplements, please **check with your doctor,** and check with your pharmacist or book an appointment with me to make sure they won't interact with any of your conditions or medications. Remember, when your provider asks for the list of medications you're currently taking, include your supplements.

These supplements will help rebuild your intestines and your intestinal microbiome to improve your digestion and decrease your symptoms. The supplements are a temporary change, you should take these for a minimum of 30 days, but 90 days is more effective. Repeat the course any time you feel your gut issues are flaring up again. This is where I started on my gut healing journey. I took them for about six months. It would have been much more effective had I removed all the poisons from my diet first. Remember to look for poisons on the labels of your supplements. Many vitamins contain them, especially gummy vitamins.

When purchasing supplements, it's important to make sure you are buying a quality brand. There is no universal regulating body for supplements. They can enter the market without testing for safety or quality so it's important to do your research here. I don't recommend specific brands. I'd rather teach you how to evaluate the products for yourself. You want to look for a few things before you make your choice.

1. Look for a third-party certificate of analysis showing purity, meaning what they say is in the bottle is actually in the bottle.
2. Look for a brand that has legitimate research supporting its effectiveness.
3. Make sure the brand is transparent about its manufacturing practices. White labeling supplements is very easy, meaning people can market a supplement as their own, but import them from countries with very low, or even no quality standards.

4. NSF International or USP stamps are helpful, but not enough. They just show that what is stated is in the bottle is actually in the bottle. They do nothing to ensure safety or effectiveness.

5. "#1 Pharmacist Recommended" or "#1 Doctor Recommended" doesn't mean anything. These labels are from polls sent out to pharmacists or doctors with incentives to win something for taking the poll. You don't know how the poll was conducted either. Were they giving a free response? Were they choosing from three options? We don't know. So don't use this as a guide.

6. Just because beautiful people are selling it on Instagram, doesn't mean it's a good choice.

Overall, just do a little research. You will be amazed what you can find in a few minutes. Or amazed at what you can't easily find and companies try to cover up. If you have difficulty finding information about a product, then it is probably not a good choice.

Let's get into the supplements for gut health. These are the ones I recommend. And, yes, I recommend all of them. They all target a slightly different aspect of your GI system and together they may even create what I like to call synergy. Synergy is one of my favorite terms in pharmacy. It means multiple things working together to create an effect that is greater than their sum. With painful digestion, we need to address all aspects of the problem from the structure of your GI system, to the microbes living in there.

We don't want to add all these supplements at once. We will add one new one every five days. That way it will give your body a few days to ensure you are not experiencing any flareups from these supplements. You should not experience flareups from these supplements if you do your research and read the full label to ensure there are no damaging substances in them (remember gummy vitamins are usually full of additives).

Collagen: Collagen is probably my favorite supplement there is. It comes in so many forms: powder, liquid, capsules, and of course my personal favorite, bone broth. The powder form you can dissolve in drinks and smoothies or hide it from your children in their homemade bars or oatmeal. Collagen doesn't just support your gut, it also supports bone, skin, hair, joint and nail health. Collagen is the main protein found in your body. It is responsible for your body's connective tissues including bone, cartilage, ligaments, tendons, skin and your gut epithelium of course. The American diet usually avoids things like tendons, skin, cartilage and ligaments. We mainly eat the muscle component of animals which only contains about 2% collagen. This is why we have to supplement collagen.

The difference between collagen powder and protein powder is their amino acid make-up. Protein powder is a general term, but usually indicates a complete protein meaning it has all the essential amino acids. Collagen is not a complete protein. You're probably thinking, "ok cool, so let's take the complete protein then, not collagen." Well, you have a damaged gut lining that needs some special care. Collagen is key to intestinal health because it is much higher in proline and glycine than typical protein powder is. Proline and glycine are the amino acids responsible for building a healthy gut lining.

According to a study in *Frontiers in Immunology,* glycine is significantly reduced in patients with inflammatory bowel disease. Glycine plays many roles in the body that include regulating behavior, body homeostasis, controlling intake of food, immune function, and plays a role in the absorption of fat-soluble vitamins. Studies have shown that glycine protects the stomach lining from damage, fights oxidative stress in the

GI tract, lowers inflammation, and modulates stomach acid secretion.

Proline is the other player here. This amino acid protects against stress and helps with nutrient adaptation. Studies have shown that proline fuels certain types of immune cells. These specialized cells are responsible for maintaining intestinal immune function. They do this by fighting harmful bacteria, maintaining the integrity of the cell wall, and controlling inflammatory cytokine secretion.

To start gaining the amazing benefits of glycine and proline, start taking a collagen supplement according to the label daily. Many options are out there. I'm not a big fan of the tablets or capsules because you usually have to take 6 or more tablets. Powder is a good place to start. It can easily be mixed into drinks, smoothies, or oatmeal. Or start drinking 8 oz of bone broth daily. I like to drink mine either in the morning or at night, kind of as my tea. For the vegetarians out there, I can't stress the importance of collagen enough. Many brands make a marine collagen now that is just as effective for gut health. Make sure you are avoiding marketing scams and reading the package label. Collagen is a big buzz word, so do your research here as you would for any other supplement.

L-Glutamine: L-glutamine is the most abundant amino acid in the body. This amino acid has been shown to be deficient in people with IBS, inflammatory bowel disease, stress, trauma, allergies, immune disorders, and those undergoing chemotherapy. L-glutamine is vital in maintaining the integrity of the intestinal wall by regulating intestinal cell proliferation. In addition, this amino acid modulates the tight junctions which keep out toxins and bacteria. L-glutamine has many studies showing it contains anti-inflammatory properties by suppressing the activation of inflammatory pathways. The turn-over rate of intestinal cells is about four to five days. Proper maintenance of cell-turnover is vital. Too much cell death is seen in inflammatory bowel disease, but too little can lead to inflammation or even things like cancer. L-glutamine helps maintain an appropriate balance of cell turn-over in the intestinal wall. Studies have shown that supplementation with L-glutamine can improve intestinal disease and keep the intestinal lining healthy. Research is still being done to determine the extent of L-glutamine's role in digestive health.

L-glutamine capsules can be found over the counter from many reputable companies. Remember to do your research. Start taking L-glutamine capsules according to the package labeling daily. Evening is best, but taking it in the morning is fine if that's when you can remember to take it.

Fish Oil: Hopefully fish oil is already a staple supplement in your repertoire. If not, it's time to add it. Fish oil is so important for your health. Fish oil contains the essential omega-3 fatty acids DHA and EPA. Essential means your body can't make it, so you must consume it. These essential fatty acids are in every cell of your body. Over 30,000 studies have been done on the role of DHA and EPA. Omega-3 fatty acids decrease inflammation by increasing the creation of short-chain fatty acids. They are also shown to increase the diversity of healthy bacteria according to an article in *International Journal of Molecular Science.* The fatty acids are also very important in the structure of cell membranes, meaning they maintain your intestinal wall integrity. So, less inflammation, increased beneficial bacteria, and improved cell wall integrity just from one little capsule. Pretty good right? And I'm just talking about gut health. I didn't even mention it lowers blood pressure, reduces overall inflammation, helps reduce anxiety and depression, and can even slow bone density and muscle loss.

You want to look for a natural, non-processed, fish or krill oil. Start taking a fish oil supplement and aim for 1000-

1500 mg DHA and EPA daily. This number is constantly changing so keep up with reputable sources of research before choosing one.

Reishi Mushrooms: The world of mushrooms is a fascinating one. Fungi makes up its own kingdom in the biology classification system. If you don't eat mushrooms on the regular, I suggest you start adding them in. Reishi is considered the Queen of Mushrooms. This powerful mushroom has a vast array of health benefits. Reishi contains triterpenes and beta-glucans which help balance the endocrine system. When the endocrine system is in balance, which very few are, the body is able to rest, restore and recover at night as it is meant to. Triterpenes are thought to be one of the best anti-inflammatory and anti-microbial compounds in nature. Triterpenes have immense benefit all over your body, from decreasing stress to containing anti-cancer properties. Beta-glucans help support your immune system. As we know, 70% of your immune system lies in your GI tract. Reishi specifically contains over 200 active ingredients making it one of the most valued longevity herbs. Interestingly, reishi is believed to be the only source of a triterpene group known as ganoderic acids. These are thought to have anti-tumor effects and strong effects on the immune system. Reishi has been used for hundreds of years in eastern medicine and has been known as the long-life herb.

Adding reishi to your supplement list can aid in rest and recovery and can help your gut rebalance and heal over time. Reishi can be found in powder or pill form at many health food stores. You can't really eat this mushroom as it is very tough. Most mushrooms are 90% water, but reishi is only 75% water. Perhaps the lack of water is to make room for all those beneficial compounds. I am a strong supporter of adaptogenic mushrooms, but too many added at once can cause diarrhea. Stick to reishi daily according to package instructions. If reishi sits well in your system then feel free to add more mushrooms to fit your health goals.

Probiotics: I am a very pro probiotic pharmacist. I feel probiotics are overlooked and can provide so much benefit. Our GI tract is full of billions of microorganisms. We've already hit this subject pretty hard in the beginning of the book, but a little review never hurts. Microorganisms can help or hinder our digestion. For those of you who were heavy on the poisons, sugar, and alcohol before you read this book, you likely have intestines full of microbes that are hindering your digestion. For those of you that feel you have worked hard to eat a healthy diet your whole life, but perhaps you've had many courses of antibiotics, especially as a young child, your intestinal microbiome is likely the cause of your GI issues.

Probiotics will help replace the bad microbes with good microbes. It's kind of like putting ladybugs in your garden. Instead of spreading poisonous pesticides all over your vegetable garden and poisoning your food, you add ladybugs to safely eat all those pests. The probiotics are your ladybugs replacing your intestinal pests with digestion enhancing microbes. The goal of this whole book is cultivating healthy microbes in your intestines. Adding the actual microbes via probiotics is a great way to kickstart that process.

Choosing the right probiotic is tricky because there are so many strains, products, and opinions out there. I recommend choosing one with a high CFU count, minimum 10-20 billion. Look for products that contain multiple strains. Look for strains that are clinically studied and brands that have proof of great results. I don't have one strain that I prefer. I like to switch it up. You can look for strains studied for your particular issue. Many studies exist and data is changing all the time, but the strains showing promise right now are: *L. reuteri* or *S. boulardii* for diarrhea, *B. lactis* for constipation, *B. infantis* and *B. acidophilus* for gas, *S. boulardii* for Crohn's and ulcerative colitis. These are only a few recommendations. Keep an eye out for emerging data.

You can get your probiotics from food such as yogurt, kombucha, sauerkraut, and kimchi, to name a few. Many foods that should contain probiotics are killed during processing, so make sure the label says "live active cultures". If you ferment your own foods or vegetables, then your gut likely has a very healthy microbiome and you probably don't need extra supplementation. You probably aren't even reading this book. Fermenting your own foods is the absolute best way to add probiotics to your diet. Not only will it help your gut, but it will help your skin and lungs as well. It's also not as hard as you might think. You can create "sourdough" oats by mixing oats and water. So, it can be pretty simple.

If you can't ferment your own foods then start taking a daily probiotic according to the package directions. You may have a slight upset stomach and bloating the first few days as things are changing. I recommend a 30 day course of probiotics a minimum of once a year as well as after every round of antibiotics of any kind.

Fiber: Many physicians believe that IBS is in part caused by lack of dietary fiber. As we have learned, high

FODMAP fiber can cause serious issues in the GI tract. But long chain, mildly fermentable fibers such as psyllium husk can improve symptoms by adding bulk and increasing peristalsis (GI movement) with very low gas production. If you suffer from loose stools often you may be thinking you definitely don't want to add fiber to speed things up even more! But fiber that adds bulk can actually improve loose stools. I know, it's counterintuitive. Look for a bulking fiber like psyllium husk and start taking a daily dose. You want to add this slowly and work your way up to 20 to 35 grams of dietary fiber daily. You can add these fibers to smoothies, oatmeal, baked goods, or just mix them into water. If you suffer from hemorrhoids and the bulking causes painful stools then lower the dose. Remember to check the label for poisons. Many fiber supplements have added sugar and artificial flavoring.

Summary: These supplements will help rebuild your gut lining and improve the microorganisms in your microbiome. We will add a new one every five days. Take the course for 30 to 90 days. Don't forget to continue your forever changes from the last section (sleep, hydration, no poisons). Continue to track your changes in your journal.

STEPS TO REBUILD

We won't add all the supplements at one time. We will add one every five days and record results in our FSJ.

DAY 31	Add daily collagen and track your results in your FSJ.
DAY 35	Add daily L-Glutamine and track your results in your FSJ.
DAY 40	Add daily fish oil and track your results in your FSJ.
DAY 45	Add daily reishi and track your results in your FSJ.
DAY 50	Add daily probiotics and track your results in your FSJ.
DAY 55	Add daily fiber slowly. Start with a low dose or even half dose. You can also consider adding it every other day. Increase every five days to reach 20-35 grams daily. Track results in your FSJ.
DAY 60	Reflect on how you feel overall. Have you found any triggers? Look back on your FSJ and see if you can find any connections between how you felt and what foods you ate the previous day.

Once you have completed 30 to 90 days of these supplements, you can stop them. You don't need to take them forever. Repeat the course anytime you have a flare up. Though, I do recommend collagen and fish oil as part of a regular supplement routine for many patients. If you have questions on an ongoing supplement routine that's right for you, it's best to ask your provider for guidance.

Chapter 7: Revitalize

Pillar 4: Stress Management and Pillar 5: Exercise

By now you should be starting to notice some changes in your symptoms and maybe have found some triggers. In this next section, we are going to take your body to the next level to help you feel your best. Remember to keep up with your supplements for a minimum of 30 days (preferably 90 days), sleep seven to eight hours every night, use your FSJ, drink lots of water, and avoid those triggers and poisons.

The stress management pillars and the exercise pillars both improve the microbiome in a similar way. Studies have shown these pillars change the microbiome independently of diet, meaning even those with a poor diet can see improvement in their gut health by incorporating these pillars. The other thing these pillars have in common, is they are forever changes. Studies which show improved microbiomes due to exercise and stress management, also show the benefits went away after exercise and stress management techniques were stopped. You must incorporate these as a lifestyle change that you continue to improve upon throughout your life.

Exercise and stress management both increase short chain fatty acid (SCFA) production. SCFAs are six or less carbon chains produced by beneficial bacteria in the colon. The three main SFCAs are butyrate, propionate, and acetate. These are produced in the colon via microbial fermentation of dietary fiber. These three compounds, butyrate, propionate, and acetate work throughout our bodies to improve our health and are quite impressive in their abilities. All three compounds play roles in inflammation, immune regulation, obesity, cardiovascular protection, diabetes, inflammatory bowel disease, constipation, cancer, and brain health.

Anti-inflammatory properties: SCFAs down regulate the expression of genes that produce cytokines, chemokines, and adhesion molecules. They also promote apoptosis, or death of senescent cells. Death of cells may sound like a bad thing, but it's a very good thing and a necessary process as we will discuss later on.

Immune Regulation: The body's immune function can get quite complicated and technical. To keep things simple, I will summarize by saying the SCFAs promote beneficial immune functions which protect the body, and down regulate immune functions that cause damage and inflammation.

Anti-obesity: SCFAs have numerous roles that decrease the risk of obesity. They have the power to control leptin secretion, which is responsible for appetite. They suppress fat synthesis in the liver and modulate genes that increase fat accumulation and appetite. One study even showed that the SCFA content of human breastmilk could prevent excess weight gain in infants.

Cardiovascular protection: The cardiovascular system is strongly affected by SCFAs. SCFAs decrease the absorption of cholesterol and decrease atherosclerotic lesions. They also decrease blood pressure and protect the heart from injury.

Liver protection: Acetate specifically decreases fat accumulation and improves liver function. Propionate protects the liver from alcohol related damage. All three SCFAs decrease gene expression related to fat synthesis in the liver.

Anti-diabetes: These molecules decrease the body's formation of sugar and improve insulin sensitivity.

Inflammatory Bowel Disease Protection: Now we're getting to gut health. These can prevent or improve Crohn's and Ulcerative Colitis symptoms by down regulating inflammatory pathways, improving the formation of tight junctions and protecting against certain infections.

Anti-constipation: Butyrate promotes mucus production and improves intestinal mobility.

Cancer: SCFAs decrease cancer risk by suppressing formation of certain cancer cells and by increasing the anti-cancer activity of cytotoxic T cells.

Brain Health: Acetate and propionate decrease cognitive impairment and suppress inflammation in the brain.

That's a lot of information I just threw at you. The point in including all that is to show that your gut health is responsible for the health of your entire body. If your gut is not functioning properly, then your whole system is feeling the effects. Your painful GI symptoms should be seen as an alarm that something is not right and taking steps to heal these symptoms will improve your overall health, not just your stomach pain.

Pillar 4: Stress Management

Stress management means both mental stress as well as physical stress. We will discuss both. In our case, physical stress means stressing your gut. It has become the norm to eat all day long, from when we wake up and start with coffee to when we relax before bed and snack on popcorn or dessert. This brings tremendous stress to your intestines and doesn't give them enough time to heal and repair. We need to allow our body and our intestines to complete the clean out cycle which occurs during sleep rather than digest food. This brings us to the concept of fasting.

Fasting

Fasting isn't as scary as it sounds. I won't be asking you to starve yourself for a week or even for a whole day. At the very least, we're just talking about limiting the hours of the day that you eat. Please check in with your provider before starting any type of fast. Children under 18, pregnant women, breastfeeding women, and those with certain medical conditions should not fast.

Fasting has been around forever. It's actually quite new that humans eat three meals a day. During hunter-gatherer days humans wouldn't eat for days at a time. Many religions around the world have used fasting as part of their religious ceremonies for hundreds of years. Really, our genes are more accustomed to fasting than they are to eating every day. In modern day, fasting is talked about in every health blog and promoted by every health expert. But the problem with fasting is, everyone has a different idea on what is the best form of fasting and everyone has a different goal in mind. Some people fast to lose weight, some to balance blood sugar, some for longevity, and some to improve their physical appearance and optimize muscle mass. We will be fasting with the goal of gut health. There are a million different names for all the different fasting methods out there, but I view them as two categories:

- **Time restricted eating:** Eating every day, but only for a certain number of hours

- **Full fast:** Not consuming anything but water for a certain number of days

Although researchers haven't agreed on what the most beneficial time-frame for fasting is, what they have agreed on is that most forms of fasting have immense health benefits. The most important benefit for our goal is getting rid of something called zombie cells, or senescent cells. Senescent cells are called zombie cells because, like zombies, they should be dead. These cells spew inflammatory compounds into the body leading to inflammation, increased risk of disease, and cancer. The new trend of eating all day long gives the cells a constant influx of food keeping them barely alive. When we fast, our body has the time and energy to clean out these zombie cells, alleviating this constant influx of inflammatory compounds. In our gut, this will lead to healing the gut lining, decreased inflammation and improved microbiome.

One study in *Microorganisms Journal* showed that multiple beneficial strains of *Lachnospiraceae* flourished during that fasting period. This strain contains anti-inflammatory properties and benefits the immune system. These strains are also shown to be low in patients with inflammatory bowel disease. Two studies have shown an increase in *Akkermansia muciniphila* after fasting. This strain helps maintain homeostasis in the gut and can decrease or prevent metabolic disorders and obesity. As discussed above, fasting also increases the production of SCFAs.

Unfortunately, fasting has recently come under scrutiny because of a poorly executed study published in 2024 that has taken over social media stating that time restricted eating increases the risk of cardiovascular death. People read the headline and automatically assume it's true because it's labeled as a research study. The results of this study are more or less meaningless. For one, the study was not peer reviewed. They used two food recall surveys as their source of data to represent eight years of eating patterns. The time restricted eating group that was shown to have an increased risk of cardiovascular death did not only have different eating patterns, but had significant differences in their lifestyle habits and comorbidities. Overall, the study contains flawed data, flawed analytics, was not peer reviewed, and should not be referenced. Moving on.

Other benefits of fasting include:

- Regulation of hormones, including insulin

- Reducing risk factors for heart disease

- Feeling more energized

- Reducing cancer risk and fighting tumor growth

- Improved cognition

- **Of course, improved gut health** by decreasing inflammation and getting rid of disease-causing cells

To focus on the goals of this book, I promote fasting because it gives your gut time to rest, rebuild and revitalize. Constant influx of food does not create a healthy environment for your gut. It is constantly working to break food down and extract the nutrients. Just like you, your gut needs time to undergo its cleaning cycle and get rid of those zombie cells.

The two types of fasting we will discuss are Time Restricted Eating and 24 Hour Fasting. You should choose the one that fits your lifestyle best. A fasting plan is something you should stick to, well, forever. For these next 30 days the no exception rule exists again. So, choose something that you can stick to.

Time Restricted Eating

Time restricted eating means you only eat for a certain number of hours each day. The plan that makes the most sense to me is one that also helps balance your circadian rhythm and of course your gut cycle. The cycle goes as follows:

- Sleep for 8 hours

- Wake up: avoid eating for at least 1 hour

- Eat all your meals and snacks in a 10 hour window

- Do not eat for a minimum of 2 hours before bed

- Go to bed

Sample schedule:
- Wake up at 5:15 am

- Work out at 5:30 am

- Eat breakfast at 7:30 am

- Snack at 10:00 am

- Lunch at noon

- Snack at 2:30 pm

- Dinner at 5:30pm

- Only water until bed

- Go to bed at 9:15 pm

For some it is difficult to wait an entire hour before eating breakfast due to needing to eat with medication or just having an early start to your work day. It's ok to start your eating window earlier if needed. It is more important to keep that two hour window before bedtime free of eating than it is the morning window.

24 Hour Fasting Once a Week

24 Hour Fasting is easier for me personally to maintain on a consistent basis than time restricted eating for many reasons. Sometimes I can't get dinner ready by 5:30 pm on work days. We also like to have dinner with friends and family who usually don't want to eat dinner that early. Choosing one day a week where I know I have to say no to dinner plans is much easier. 24 hour fasting is pretty easy to follow. You only consume water for 24 hours. This doesn't mean you have to go an entire day without eating. What I do is eat breakfast and then I don't eat again until breakfast the next day. I get a lot of questions about if a certain food breaks a fast because they read an article that says x, y, or z actually doesn't break your fast. Well, whatever the x, y, or z is, if it's anything other than water, black coffee or tea, then it breaks

133

your fast in the gut health world. The schedule is pretty straight forward:

- Wake up

- Eat breakfast

- Only consume water (and black coffee or tea if you must)

- Go to bed

- Eat breakfast the next morning and eat your normal snacks and meals until the next 24 hour period the next week

Let's move on to meditation. We will discuss the steps to fasting and meditation all together at the end of the chapter.

Meditation

We can't ignore our mental stress. In addition to everything we've already discussed in this book, GI issues can stem from stress, anxiety, and depression. The gut and brain are intimately related. If we just think about food, our brain signals our gut to start secreting digestive juices. Do you feel nauseated when you have a stressful event coming up such as a presentation? Do you feel "butterflies" when you get excited about something? These are all signs of the gut brain connection. Unfortunately, anxiety, stress, and depression can cause GI issues such as diarrhea, constipation, and heartburn. Surprisingly, an unhealthy gut can also be the cause of anxiety, stress, and depression.

Perhaps some of you are like me, and didn't experience digestive issues until after a major life event. Traumatic events can alter our genes. This falls under the category of epigenetics. *The Body Keeps the Score* by Bessel Van Der Kolk, M.D. discusses how the body is altered after traumatic experiences. My body was altered in my gut and I had to take time to heal to reverse these changes. You don't have to experience trauma to have your gene expression change and gut health change. The changes can also be caused by chronic stress, anxiety and depression.

Meditation provides amazing benefits to the body and mind. Meditation for just a few minutes a day can increase your lifespan, decrease risk of disease, decrease stress, decrease anxiety, help with feelings of depression, and even change your gut microbiome. That's right, studies have found that those who meditate have a healthier gut microbiome.

Pretty amazing right? And we already know that a healthy gut microbiome is key to relieving your symptoms.

Now, you don't have to become a monk and sit on the top of a mountain and meditate for six hours at a time. You just need to add in a few minutes of meditation every day. I'm talking five minutes to start. It's probably going to be really hard to find five free minutes in your day. But, considering the average person spends over 2.5 hours on social media every day (some studies have shown nine hours a day on social media), I have faith in you. If you have never meditated before, there are lots of apps you can use to help you learn. The three most popular are Headspace, Calm, and Healthy Minds Program. There are thousands of free guided meditations online. Search for a meditation that aligns with what you are struggling with. For example, search for meditation for stress, or meditation for depression. You can also just do something as simple as set a timer and sit quietly with your eyes closed.

We are going to work our way up from five minutes of meditation to 20 minutes of meditation. I understand 20 minutes is a little harder to fit in than five minutes. If you can do it, great! If you can't, then do the bare minimum of five or whatever amount of time your schedule allows that day. You can even do this in your car in the parking lot before you head in to work or on your lunch break. I used to do it on the train on my way to grad school. Wherever you can find the time. You don't have to be in a yoga room with healing crystals in each corner. Again, we will discuss all these steps together at the end of the chapter.

Pillar 5: Movement

I'm not going to give you an intense exercise program. That's not the point of this book. I am going to tell you that movement is key to a healthy gut and a healthy mind. Remember how those things are connected? If you already have an exercise program where you are moving your body for 150 minutes per week plus doing two days of strength training, great. Keep doing that. If you don't, then it's time to make a change.

Why is exercise vital to a healthy gut? Studies show that moderate exercise decreases intestinal inflammation and permeability while increasing diversity of the good microbes in the gut. Multiple studies have found that exercise alone improved the microbiome of the subjects and increased the production of anti-inflammatory molecules. In addition, studies have also found that once exercise is stopped for a six-week period or more these benefits are reversed. You know what that means? Exercise is another one of those forever changes. The Department of Health and Human Services recommends the following:

- Moderate activity for 150 minutes per week PLUS 2 days of strength training

Or

- Vigorous activity for 75 minutes per week PLUS 2 days of strength training

The more intense it is, the less you have to do. Moderate activity means you are breathing hard, but you can carry on a conversation. Vigorous activity means your heart rate is high and you can't say more than a few words without needing to pause to breathe. Strength training should involve upper body, lower body, and core work. I'm not asking you to run the next Iron Man or follow David Goggins' foot steps, I'm just asking you to do the bare minimum recommended for basic health. The good news is some things you already do around the house count as moderate activity such as mowing the lawn or cleaning the house. There are so many things you can do to get moving, the sky's the limit. Join a gym. Most gyms offer a few personal training sessions for free upon joining. Join a local walking, running, or cycling group. You can find these through Facebook or community centers. Do all those projects your spouse has asked you to do for years.

If you are a very sedentary person let's start with baby steps. Start with a short walk daily that increases your heart rate slightly. If walking for ten minutes is all you can manage, then start with ten minutes and work your way up to thirty minutes. If you need help getting started visit health.gov's activity planner at https://health.gov/moveyourway/activity-planner. This planner will help you find activities and create a plan to meet the exercise recommendations.

Examples of moderate exercise:	Examples of vigorous exercise:	Examples of strength training:
• Walking • Riding a bike on an easy path • Mowing the lawn • Cleaning the house • Home improvement projects • Gardening • Pickleball • Doubles tennis • Golfing without a cart • Tai chi • Dancing • Playing with your kids outside • Hiking • Hot ashtanga yoga • Anything that slightly raises your heart rate and respiratory rate	• Power walking with hills • Power walking with a stroller • Cycling/riding a bike on a difficult path with hills • HIIT workouts • Running • Basketball • Soccer • Singles tennis • Vigorous hiking with elevation gain	• Lifting weights • Ashtanga Yoga • Using resistance bands • Body weight exercises

The only thing I'm going to add to the recommendations is yoga. Yoga is great for gut health. It can calm the mind and calm the gut. Certain poses that involve twisting can improve digestion, gas, bloating, and constipation. Yoga doesn't have to be difficult. You can choose a restorative style or a yin style that is very slow, relaxing and enjoyable. Adding just 10 minutes three days a week can improve your symptoms. You can find thousands of free yoga classes online. Just search for "yoga for digestion" or "restorative yoga" or "yin yoga" and you will find many short practices that can fit into your day. This can be part of your 150 minutes of exercise per week.

STEPS
TO
REVITALIZE

Step 1: Choose your fasting method and continue without exception for 30 days.

Step 2: Download a meditation app or bookmark some free guided meditations or meditation music.

Step 3: Write a workout schedule for the next 30 days that meets the recommendations. Or start off very slow if you are very new to exercise. Remember to visit https://health.gov/moveyourway/activity-planner if you need some help. You can split up the 150 minutes any way that works for you and do the strength training on the same days as cardio to allow yourself rest days. Remember to add your 10 minutes of yoga three days per week.

30 DAY PLAN

TIME RESTRICTED EATING

If you are choosing the Time Restricted Eating fasting method, then follow this plan. If you are choosing 24 Hour Fasting then go to the next page.

DAY 61 - 67	• Start your workout routine • Eat within a 10 hour window • Meditate for 5 minutes
DAY 68 - 74	• Continue workout routine. Think about the next five days. Are you ready to step things up? • Eat within a 10 hour window • Meditate for 10 minutes
DAY 75 - 81	• Continue your workout routine. Perhaps increase the intensity if you're feeling up to it. • Eat within a 10 hour window • Meditate for 15 minutes
DAY 82 - 90	• Continue your workouts. Ready to step it up? Turn that walk into a power walk? Add that big hill to the route? Bump up your weights by 5 lbs? • Eat within a 10 hour window • Meditate for 20 minutes

30 DAY PLAN
24 HOUR FASTING

If you are choosing 24 hour fasting, then follow the plan below.

DAYS 61 - 65	DAY 66
• Start your workout routine • Eat normal • Meditate for 5 minutes	• Continue your workout routine. Consider making this your rest day. • Eat breakfast only then water the rest of the day • Meditate for 5 minutes

DAY 67	DAYS 68 - 72
• Continue your workout routine. Perhaps increase the intensity if you're feeling up to it. • Break your fast with breakfast and then eat normally • Meditate for 5 minutes	• Continue your workout routine. • Eat normally • Meditate for 10 minutes

DAY 73	DAY 74
• Continue your workout routine • Eat breakfast only then water the rest of the day • Meditate for 10 minutes	• Continue your workout routine. • Break your fast with breakfast and then eat normally • Meditate for 10 minutes

DAYS 75 - 79	DAY 80
• Continue your workout routine. Bump up those weights. Consider moving your power walk to a jog. • Eat normally • Meditate for 20 minutes (or that maximum you can fit in)	• Continue your workout routine • Eat breakfast only then water the rest of the day • Meditate for 15 minutes

DAY 81	DAYS 22-88
• Continue your workout routine. • Break your fast with breakfast and then eat normally • Meditate for 15 minutes	• Continue your workout routine. Ready to step it up? Perhaps turn that walk into a power walk? Add the big hill in your area to the route? Bump up weights by 5 lbs? • Eat normally • Meditate for 15 minutes

DAY 89	DAY 90
• Continue your workout routine • Eat breakfast only then water the rest of the day • Meditate for 20 minutes	• Continue your workout routine. • Break your fast with breakfast and then eat normally • Meditate for 20 minutes

143

How do you feel after 30 days of meditation, fasting, and movement? Amazing? Less symptoms? Record your thoughts in your FSJ. Keep up this routine. Your gut, mind and aging body will thank you.

Chapter 8: Review

Restore

Step 1: Give yourself the opportunity to sleep 7 to 8 hours every night.

Step 2: Go through your kitchen, read all your food labels and eliminate everything that contains a poison. If you have a hard time letting go, think about your premature death and pain. That might help.

Step 3: Sequester all the irritants and optional irritants. Don't throw these away as we will be slowly adding them back in later.

Step 4: Stay hydrated. Start each day with a glass of water and drink water throughout the day.

Step 5: After 14 days of elimination, you can add one irritant back in every three days and record your symptoms. If you find a trigger, eliminate that food for 90 days to allow healing. Then try again.

Steps to Restore

30 DAYS TO RESTORE

DAY 1	Start the full elimination diet of poisons, irritants, and optional irritants (food chart on following pages). Remember to use your FSJ daily.
DAY 2 TO DAY 14	Hold strong on your elimination diet. It will be hard, but I know you can do it. Remember to drink lots of water.
DAY 15	Add one irritant back in and record the results over the next two days in your FSJ. If you have digestive issues flare up, eliminate that food for 90 days then try again.
DAY 18	Add another irritant and record results. Note: I don't recommend adding coffee and alcohol back in the same week as they are both strong irritants.
DAY 21	Add another irritant and record results.
DAY 24	Add another irritant and record results.
DAY 27	Add another irritant and record results.
DAY 30	Add another irritant and record results. You made it! Congratulations! How do you feel? Did you feel like garbage sometimes and blame me for your pain? Thats okay. Now you can thank me when you don't run to the bathroom three times on your next date.

Poisons

FOOD GUIDE: POISONS

Poisons Eliminate Permanently		Healthy Replacements	
Oils/Fats		Oils/Fats	
• Processed fat including trans fat and non-butter spreads • Canola oil • Soybean oil	• Corn oil • Grapeseed oil • Safflower oil • "Vegetable oil" • Cottonseed oil • Sunflower oil	• Animal fats • Olive oil • Peanut oil	• Butter • Palm oil • Coconut oil
Added Sugar Sweeteners		Foods that are naturally sweet such as fresh or frozen fruit	
Artificial/Chemicals		Natural	
• Fat free • Artificial sweeteners • Artificial flavor • Buzzword junk food • Aspartame • Sucralose • Acesulfame K • Saccharin • Aluminum • Nitrites	• Nitrites • Nitrates • Potassium bromate • Propyl Paraben • BHA • Propyl gallate • Theobromine • Artificial coloring • Diacetyl • Phosphates • Many more	• Full fat products (rather than fat free or low fat) • Nitrate free meats • Natural flavoring	
Junk Food		Whole, Non-Processed Foods	
• Fast food • Candy • Ice cream • Frozen yogurt • Fried food • Processed food • Sugary cereal • Most snack bars • Juice • Syrup	• Pastries • Cookies • Cake • Cupcakes • Pancakes • Whipped topping • Flavored oatmeal • Waffles • Muffins • Jelly/jam	• Cook at home • Do your research on your favorite restaurants • Meat • Eggs • Oatmeal • Vegetables • Fruit • Full fat dairy	• Homemade whipped cream with no sugar added • Homemade smoothies • Nuts/seeds • Peanut Butter • Quinoa • Wild rice

147

FOOD GUIDE: IRRITANTS

Irritants Eliminate for 14 Days	Healthy Replacements
Wheat, Barley, Rye, Gluten	Starches/Grains
• Pasta • Bread • Crackers • Cereal • Bars • Desserts • Many more	• Potatoes • Wild Rice • Sweet potatoes • Lentils • Oatmeal • Beans • Quinoa
Coffee	Green Tea
Chocolate/Cacao/Cacao Nibs	Other antioxidants or crunchy toppings such as berries and nuts
• Garlic • Onions • Spicy	• Turmeric • Mustard • Cumin powder • Cinnamon • Lemon pepper • Cardamom • Paprika • Allspice • Smoked paprika
Liquid Dairy	Plant based milk with no added oils or poisons
Alcohol • Beer • Mixed Drinks • Wine • Seltzers • Hard liquor	• Water • Tea • Sparkling water • Shrubs (vinegar based drink)
Sweeteners • Sorbitol • Monk fruit • Xylitol • Many others • Stevia	Naturally Sweet Foods • Fruit
High FODMAPs (listed below)	Low FODMAPs Medium FODMAPs in small quantities

Optional Irritants
• All caffeine   • Peppermint
• Tomatoes/tomato   • All peppers
  sauce   • Oatmeal
• Citrus   • All Dairy
• Black pepper   • Eggs
• Bacon/sausage   • Medium FODMAP
	• Herbal tea • Oats soaked
	• Quinoa overnight
	• Wild rice • Low FODMAPs
	• Sweet potatoes
	• Try new spices
	• Non-carbonated
	  drinks

FODMAPs

FOOD GUIDE: FODMAPS

High FODMAPs		Low FODMAPs	
Fruit		**Fruit**	
• Apples	• Mangoes	• Banana	• Lemons
• Apricots	• Nectarines	• Blueberries	• Limes
• Blackberries	• Peaches	• Cantaloupe	• Mandarin
• Boysenberries	• Pears	• Clementine	• Orange
• Cherries	• Persimmons	• Coconut	• Papaya
• Currants	• Plums	• Dragon fruit	• Passion fruit
• Dates	• Prunes	• Grapes	• Pineapple
• Figs	• Tamarillo	• Guava	• Raspberries
• Grapefruit	• Watermelon	• Honeydew	• Rhubarb
		• Kiwifruit	• Strawberries
Vegetables and Legumes		**Vegetables and Legumes**	
• Artichokes	• Garlic	• Arugula	• Okra
• Asparagus	• Shallots	• Bamboo	• Nori seaweed
• Cauliflower	• Beans	• Bok Choy	• Spaghetti Squash
• Garlic	• Peas	• Bell Peppers	• Spinach
• Leeks	• Snap peas	• Carrots	• Olives
• Mushrooms	• Snow peas	• Chives	• Parsnips
• Onion	• Soybeans	• Collard greens	• Potatoes
		• Cabbages	• Radishes
Grains		• Chilis	• Scallions
• Rye	• Wheat	• Cucumber	• Squash
• Barley		• Eggplant	• Swiss chard
		• Endive	• Tomatoes
Protein		• Fennel	• Turnips
• Silken Tofu		• Ginger	• Watercress
		• Green beans	• Water Chestnuts
Other		• Kale	• Zucchini
• Pistachios	• Chicory root	• Leeks	
• Cashews	• Chamomile tea	• Lettuce	
• Cottage cheese	• Fennel tea		
• Milk Yogurt	• Oolong tea	**Grains**	
• Agave	• Inulin	• Rice	• Oats
• Honey		• Buckwheat	• Polenta
		• Cornmeal	• Quinoa
		• Corn flour	• Tapioca
		• Millet	
		Protein	
		• Animal based: grass fed beef, pork, fish, free range chicken, etc.	• Firm tofu
			• Tempeh

149

Rebuild

STEPS TO REBUILD

We won't add all the supplements at one time. We will add one every five days and record results in our FSJ.

DAY 31	Add daily collagen and track your results in your FSJ.
DAY 35	Add daily L-Glutamine and track your results in your FSJ.
DAY 40	Add daily fish oil and track your results in your FSJ.
DAY 45	Add daily reishi and track your results in your FSJ.
DAY 50	Add daily probiotics and track your results in your FSJ.
DAY 55	Add daily fiber slowly. Start with a low dose or even half dose. You can also consider adding it every other day. Increase every five days to reach 20-35 grams daily. Track results in your FSJ.
DAY 60	Reflect on how you feel overall. Have you found any triggers? Look back on your FSJ and see if you can find any connections between how you felt and what foods you ate the previous day.

STEPS
TO
REVITALIZE

Step 1: Choose your fasting method and continue without exception for 30 days.

Step 2: Download a meditation app or bookmark some free guided meditations or meditation music.

Step 3: Write a workout schedule for the next 30 days that meets the recommendations. Or start off very slow if you are very new to exercise. Remember to visit https://health.gov/moveyourway/activity-planner if you need some help. You can split up the 150 minutes any way that works for you and do the strength training on the same days as cardio to allow yourself rest days. Remember to add your 10 minutes of yoga three days per week.

30 DAY PLAN
TIME RESTRICTED EATING

If you are choosing the Time Restricted Eating fasting method, then follow this plan. If you are choosing 24 Hour Fasting then go to the next page.

DAY 61 - 67	• Start your workout routine • Eat within a 10 hour window • Meditate for 5 minutes
DAY 68 - 74	• Continue workout routine. Think about the next five days. Are you ready to step things up? • Eat within a 10 hour window • Meditate for 10 minutes
DAY 75 - 81	• Continue your workout routine. Perhaps increase the intensity if you're feeling up to it. • Eat within a 10 hour window • Meditate for 15 minutes
DAY 82 - 90	• Continue your workouts. Ready to step it up? Turn that walk into a power walk? Add that big hill to the route? Bump up your weights by 5 lbs? • Eat within a 10 hour window • Meditate for 20 minutes

30 DAY PLAN
24 HOUR FASTING

If you are choosing 24 hour fasting, then follow the plan below.

DAYS 61 - 65	DAY 66
• Start your workout routine • Eat normal • Meditate for 5 minutes	• Continue your workout routine. Consider making this your rest day. • Eat breakfast only then water the rest of the day • Meditate for 5 minutes

DAY 67	DAYS 68 - 72
• Continue your workout routine. Perhaps increase the intensity if you're feeling up to it. • Break your fast with breakfast and then eat normally • Meditate for 5 minutes	• Continue your workout routine. • Eat normally • Meditate for 10 minutes

DAY 73	DAY 74
• Continue your workout routine • Eat breakfast only then water the rest of the day • Meditate for 10 minutes	• Continue your workout routine. • Break your fast with breakfast and then eat normally • Meditate for 10 minutes

DAYS 75 - 79	DAY 80
• Continue your workout routine. Bump up those weights. Consider moving your power walk to a jog. • Eat normally • Meditate for 20 minutes (or that maximum you can fit in)	• Continue your workout routine • Eat breakfast only then water the rest of the day • Meditate for 15 minutes

DAY 81	DAYS 22-88
• Continue your workout routine. • Break your fast with breakfast and then eat normally • Meditate for 15 minutes	• Continue your workout routine. Ready to step it up? Perhaps turn that walk into a power walk? Add the big hill in your area to the route? Bump up weights by 5 lbs? • Eat normally • Meditate for 15 minutes

DAY 89	DAY 90
• Continue your workout routine • Eat breakfast only then water the rest of the day • Meditate for 20 minutes	• Continue your workout routine. • Break your fast with breakfast and then eat normally • Meditate for 20 minutes

154

Chapter 9: Reflect

Congratulations! Over the last 90 days you have restored, rebuilt, and revitalized your gut. Now it's time to reflect on your journey. If you made it through all 90 days you should be very proud of yourself. You should also be feeling like you and your toilet are no longer as close as you used to be.

Get out your F&S Journal and write down the following:

- What foods are triggers? Avoid these for at least 90 days.

- What changes were the hardest for you?

- What symptoms have improved?

- What activities are you now able to do that you couldn't before?

- Are you able to continue the forever changes (no poisons, lots of water, fasting, meditation, exercise and yoga)? If not, how can you slightly modify them, but still gain some benefit (for example maybe only meditate for 5 minutes a day instead of 20, or only fast for 24 hours every 30 days instead of every 7)?

- How do you feel overall after completing this journey?

Did you perhaps, maybe, kind of, just a little bit not make it through all 90 days? That's understandable. These aren't easy changes to make. It took me over 10 years to figure all this out for myself. I wish someone could have told me how to do it in 90 days. Get out your F&S Journal and go through the bullet points above as well as the following:

- What was the most difficult part of this for you?

- List all the reasons you weren't able to complete all 90 days

- Next to each reason, list a way you can modify it to work for you

- List out all your symptoms and next to each symptom list how it hinders your life

- List out reasons you want to feel better

- Come up with a date you want to give this another try

Did you go through all 90 days but your symptoms haven't changed as much as you were hoping? If this is the case, book a private appointment with me and we can discuss your personal situation. Everyone is different. I'll list some reasons and additional actions you can take that may help.

- Have you not seen your doctor lately? Visit your doctor to make sure you don't have any underlying health issues. In addition to your primary care provider (not in place of), consider seeing a naturopath. They tend to do more in depth blood work that can find specific nutrient problems.

- It's possible the food that affects you is not one of the typical irritants. You can order a food sensitivity test online. You should also consider visiting an allergist to see if you have a true allergy to a certain food. Consider eliminating the following foods for 14 to 30 days:

157

- All dairy

- Soy

- Nightshades: bell peppers, tomatoes, eggplant, potatoes

- Red meat

- Meat/fish treated with antibiotics

- Genetically Modified Organisms (GMO): most common are wheat, soy and corn

- Your gut may be very damaged and you may need longer to heal. Consider repeating the Diet Restoration phase and do the following:

  o Increase the elimination phase from 14 days to 30 days

  o Add one food back every 7 days

  o Add coffee last to give your body a longer break and start with every other day rather than every day

- Keep alcohol out of your diet for as long as possible

Did you maybe cheat a little? Only you know if you did. Was it just too hard to give up coffee? Or was it too hard to give up alcohol? Or too hard to give up that fast food restaurant filled with poisons? Maybe you don't believe me that coffee is an irritant. If you didn't complete the elimination phase in its entirety, then consider repeating it without cheating. Or, at the bare minimum consider removing that one hard-to-let-go-of item for 14 days and see how you feel. We're not aiming for perfection, just improvement. You can take baby steps if that works better for you.

Do you take lots of medications or lots of supplements? Both of these things can lead to digestive issues. If this is the case then book a private appointment with me and we can discuss some options for you personally.

Hopefully this journey has brought you some relief in your symptoms and helped you identify some of the causes. I encourage you to keep the poisons out of your diet as much as possible. I also encourage you to continue your fasting, water, meditation, and exercise routines. These changes will continue to not only support your gut health, but support your overall health and ease the pain of aging. It's normal to have setbacks and fall off your routine sometimes. That's okay, we're all human. When this happens, evaluate where you're at and where you would like to be. Start making small changes every day to get back to a place of balance and health to feel your best.

Conclusion

As we come to the end of *Guide Your Gut,* it is clear that
the health of our gut and microbiome is directly correlated to
our overall health. Your painful digestive symptoms should be
seen as a warning alarm from your body telling you
something is not right. They should not be ignored and
dismissed as "a tummy ache" and they should not be covered
up with drugs which are causing even more problems. Our
gut is our first line of defense against the substances you bring
into your body. We need our gut lining to be strong and our
microbiome to be healthy and diverse in order for our bodies
to function properly.

As we learned, digestive issues are a result of both
physical damage of the gut lining and improper balance of
beneficial and harmful microbes. Healing the microbial
makeup of your gut goes hand and hand with healing the
damaged physical properties of your gut. Physical damage
can include damage to the mucus layer, damage to the tight
junctions, and damage to the enterocytes themselves. These

injuries disrupt the function of your gut leading to painful cramping, diarrhea, constipation, and heartburn. These injuries also create buildup of inflammatory molecules and allow passage of large molecules and pathogens into your body. Once these toxic substances and pathogens enter your body, it can cause a cascade of health issues. Most people with gut issues also suffer from things like brain fog, fatigue, skin issues, weight gain, and even more serious ailments like chronic inflammation.

Your microbial balance can be disrupted by antibiotic use, poor diet, dehydration, lack of sleep, chronic stress, trauma, depression, and lack of exercise. This imbalance can lead to the physical damage discussed above, as well as gas, bloating, cramping, diarrhea, constipation, heartburn, and chronic inflammation. And similar to above, a disrupted microbiome can cascade into health issues all over the body. The microbial makeup of your gut can control your food cravings, your digestion, your ability to uptake important nutrients, the pathogens that enter your body, your level of inflammation, and your immune system function. The larger a colony of bacteria is, the stronger its effect is on your body and brain. Large colonies send stronger signals to your brain telling it what foods to crave. Larger colonies can also push out beneficial bacteria compounding the problem.

around fear and anxiety everywhere I go, which is very liberating.

I know you are likely in a dark place right now with your symptoms running your life. I know the feeling. I was there too and I didn't think I would ever get better. But you can get better and you have the power to do it yourself. You don't need the drug companies to give you more pills and take more of your money. You need to take the time to care for your body and heal. I hope reading this book will help you not feel alone in your pain and give you hope that you will heal! Remember, small changes add up. Take baby steps if you have to, because over time, they will make a difference. Make conscious decisions to support balance and health by paying attention to your body's needs and listening to its signals. You can do this!

References

1. Lee YB, Byun EJ, Kim HS. Potential Role of the Microbiome in Acne: A Comprehensive Review. *Journal of Clinical Medicine*. 2019; 8(7):987. https://doi.org/10.3390/jcm8070987

2. Xiao J, Grier A, Faustoferri RC, et al. Association between Oral Candida and Bacteriome in Children with Severe ECC. *Journal of Dental Research*. 2018;97(13):1468-1476. doi:10.1177/0022034518790941

3. Lindsay M. Kindinger *et al.*
4. ,Relationship between vaginal microbial dysbiosis, inflammation, and pregnancy outcomes in cervical cerclage.*Sci. Transl. Med.***8**,350ra102-350ra102(2016).DOI:10.1126/scitranslmed.aag1026

5. Koochakpoor G, Salari-Moghaddam A, Keshteli AH, Esmaillzadeh A, Adibi P. Association of Coffee and Caffeine Intake With Irritable Bowel Syndrome in Adults. Front Nutr. 2021 Jun 15;8:632469. doi: 10.3389/fnut.2021.632469. PMID: 34211993; PMCID: PMC8241212.

6. Bertrand, Julien, et al. "Glutamine Restores Tight Junction Protein Claudin-1 Expression in Colonic Mucosa of Patients with Diarrhea-Predominant Irritable Bowel Syndrome." JPEN. Journal of Parenteral and Enteral Nutrition, vol. 40, no. 8, 1 Nov. 2016, pp. 1170–1176, pubmed.ncbi.nlm.nih.gov/25972430/, https://doi.org/10.1177/0148607115587330. Accessed 19 May 2021.

7. Cederbaum, Arthur I. "Alcohol Metabolism." Clinics in Liver Disease, vol. 16, no. 4, Nov. 2012, pp. 667–685, https://doi.org/10.1016/j.cld.2012.08.002.

8. Xheng, Xiaowen, et al. "The role of amino acid metabolism in inflammatory bowel disease and other inflammatory disease." Frontiers in Immunology, vol. 14, 22 October 2023, https://doi.org/10.3389/fimmu.2023.1284133.

9. Costantini L, Molinari R, Farinon B, Merendino N. Impact of Omega-3 Fatty Acids on the Gut Microbiota. Int J Mol Sci. 2017 Dec 7;18(12):2645. doi: 10.3390/ijms18122645. PMID: 29215589; PMCID: PMC5751248.

10. Clauss, Matthieu, et al. "Interplay between Exercise and Gut Microbiome in the Context of Human Health and Performance." Frontiers in Nutrition, vol. 8, no. 8, 10 June 2021, https://doi.org/10.3389/fnut.2021.637010.

11. El-Salhy, Magdy, et al. "Dietary Fiber in Irritable Bowel Syndrome (Review)." International Journal of Molecular Medicine, vol. 40, no. 3, 19 July 2017, pp. 607–613, www.ncbi.nlm.nih.gov/pmc/articles/PMC5548066/, https://doi.org/10.3892/ijmm.2017.3072.

12. Gorgoulis, Vassilis, et al. "Cellular Senescence: Defining a Path Forward." Cell, vol. 179, no. 4, Oct. 2019, pp. 813–827, www.cell.com/cell/fulltext/S0092-8674(19)31121-3, https://doi.org/10.1016/j.cell.2019.10.005.

13. Gwak, Min-Gyu, and Sun-Young Chang. "Gut-Brain Connection: Microbiome, Gut Barrier, and Environmental Sensors." Immune Network, vol. 21, no. 3, 2021, https://doi.org/10.4110/in.2021.21.e20.

14. Kim, Min-Hyun, and Hyeyoung Kim. "The Roles of Glutamine in the Intestine and Its Implication in Intestinal Diseases." International Journal of Molecular Sciences, vol. 18, no. 5, 12 May 2017, p. 1051, www.ncbi.nlm.nih.gov/pmc/articles/PMC5454963/.

15. Liang, Xinwen, et al. "Proline Mechanisms of Stress Survival." Antioxidants & Redox Signaling, vol. 19, no. 9, 20 Sept. 2013, pp. 998–1011, www.ncbi.nlm.nih.gov/pmc/articles/PMC3763223/, https://doi.org/10.1089/ars.2012.5074.

16. Manoogian, Emily N C, et al. "Time-Restricted Eating for the Prevention and Management of Metabolic Diseases." Endocrine Reviews, vol. 43, no. 2, 22 Sept. 2021, https://doi.org/10.1210/endrev/bnab027.

17. Melissa Hartwig Urban. Cooking Whole30. Houghton Mifflin, 1 Dec. 2020.

18. Menni, Cristina, et al. "Omega-3 Fatty Acids Correlate with Gut Microbiome Diversity and Production of N-Carbamylglutamate in Middle Aged and Elderly Women." Scientific Reports, vol. 7, no. 1, 11 Sept. 2017, pp. 1–11, www.nature.com/articles/s41598-017-10382-2, https://doi.org/10.1038/s41598-017-10382-2.

19. ND Julie Briley, and ND Courtney Jackson. Food as Medicine Everyday. Nunm Press, 14 Sept. 2016.

20. Nichols, Lily. Real Food for Pregnancy : The Science and Wisdom of Optimal Prenatal Nutrition. United States?, Lily Nichols, 2018.

21. Noveille, Agatha. The Complete Guide to Adaptogens : From Ashwagandha to Rhodiola, Medicinal Herbs That Transform and Heal. New York, Adams Media, 2018.

22. Razak, Meerza Abdul, et al. "Multifarious Beneficial Effect of Nonessential Amino Acid, Glycine: A Review." Oxidative Medicine and Cellular Longevity, vol. 2017, no. 8, 2017, pp. 1–8, https://doi.org/10.1155/2017/1716701.

23. Sathish Kumar Natarajan, et al. "Proline Dehydrogenase Is Essential for Proline Protection against Hydrogen Peroxide-Induced Cell Death." Free Radical Biology and Medicine, vol. 53, no. 5, 1 Sept.

2012, pp. 1181–1191, https://doi.org/10.1016/j.freeradbiomed.2012.07.002. Accessed 28 Apr. 2023.

24. Scarlata, Kate, and Dede Wilson. The Low-FODMAP Diet Step by Step. Da Capo Lifelong Books, 19 Dec. 2017.

25. Shanahan, Catherine, and Luke Shanahan. Deep Nutrition : Why Your Genes Need Traditional Food. New York, Flatiron Books, 2018.

26. T, Michael, and Pizzorno Joseph Murray. The Encyclopedia of Natural Medicine Third Edition. Atria Books, 2012.

27. Tero Isokauppila, and Mark H Hyman. Healing Mushrooms : A Practical and Culinary Guide to Using Mushrooms for Whole Body Health. New York, New York, Avery, An Imprint Of Penguin Random House, 2017.

28. Walker, Matthew P. Why We Sleep : Unlocking the Power of Sleep and Dreams. New York, Ny, Scribner, An Imprint Of Simon & Schuster, Inc, 2017.

29. Xiong RG, Zhou DD, Wu SX, Huang SY, Saimaiti A, Yang ZJ, Shang A, Zhao CN, Gan RY, Li HB. Health Benefits and Side Effects of Short-Chain Fatty Acids. Foods. 2022 Sep 15;11(18):2863. doi: 10.3390/foods11182863. PMID: 36140990; PMCID: PMC9498509.

About the Author

Kristen Fincham, PharmD, MS, BCGP

Kristen has a doctorate in pharmacology from USC, a masters in Health Care Decision Analysis from USC, and a bachelors in Food Science Technology from Oregon State. She also holds a board specialty certification in geriatric pharmacy. Her job as a clinical pharmacist is to understand the ins and outs of human physiology, how substances (such as drugs, food, or chemicals) affect the body, how the body affects these substances, and how multiple substances within the body affect each other. Her education in food science combined with her understanding of physiology give her a unique perspective on how the modern day diet and food processing is interacting with the human body. She considers the gut as the centerpiece of our health and is dedicated to helping patients heal their gut to heal their body. Through her business, MedFreePharmD, she has helped patients reclaim their health and get their life back.

Printed in Great Britain
by Amazon

46535588R00096